P9-DVQ-100

do it NOW *do it* FAST *do it* RIGHT®

Garage
Solutions

do it NOW *do it* FAST *do it* RIGHT®

Garage
Solutions

The Taunton Press

Text ©2005 by The Taunton Press, Inc.

Photographs by John Rickard, Jerry Bates, and Robert J. Dolezal ©2005 by The Taunton Press, Inc.

Illustrations ©2005 by The Taunton Press, Inc.

All rights reserved.

The Taunton Press, Inc., 63 South Main Street, PO Box 5506, Newtown, CT 06470-5506

e-mail: tp@taunton.com

PRODUCED BY Dolezal & Associates

WRITER: Rich Binsacca

PROJECT MANAGER: Robert J. Dolezal

SERIES DESIGN: Lori Wendin

LAYOUT: Barbara K. Dolezal

ILLUSTRATOR: Charles Lockhart, Lockhart Art & Design

PHOTOSHOP ARTIST: Jerry Bates

PHOTOGRAPHER: John Rickard

COVER PHOTOGRAPHER: John Rickard, except back cover (third from top) courtesy Gladiator GarageWorks

Taunton's Do It Now/Do It Fast/Do It Right® is a trademark of The Taunton Press, Inc., registered in the U.S. Patent and Trademark Office.

LIBRARY OF CONGRESS CATALOGING-IN-PUBLICATION DATA

Garage solutions.

    p. cm. -- (Do it now/do it fast/do it right)

 ISBN 1-56158-760-5

 1. Garages--Remodeling--Amateurs' manuals. 2. Storage in the home--Amateurs' manuals. I. Taunton Press. II. Series.

 TH4960.G39 2005

 648' .8--dc22

                      2004028044

Printed in the United States of America

10 9 8 7 6 5 4 3 2 1

The following manufacturers/names appearing in *Garage Solutions* are trademarks: A&W®, Ace™, All Bright Ideas™, Better Life Technologies™, Black & Decker®, Bulls Eye™, Cannondale®, Cat®, Coke®, Craftsman™, Custom®, DeWalt™, Diamond®, Dr. Pepper®, Elmer's™, Farrari™, Fat Max, Fire Storm™, Flexall®, Garage Tek®, Gladiator GarageWorks™, Griot's Garage®, Hanson®, Home Focus®, Hyloft®, Improvements®, IronClad®, JM™ Johns Manville, K2®, Le Croix®, Liquid Nails™, Lufkin®, Minwax™, Mountain Dew®, Mylec®,

Acknowledgments

We're grateful to the homeowners, businesses, workers, consultants, associations, and experts whose talent and hard work helped make this book possible. Thanks to the following individuals and families: Lindsay Archer, Jacques Bleisae, and Tory Shannon. Thanks also to the following manufacturers and retailers for generously supplying photographs and products: All Bright Ideas, Better Life Technologies, Garage Tek, Gladiator GarageWorks, Griot's Garage, Home Focus Catalog, Hyloft, Improvements Catalog, Lighting Universe, Northern Tool & Equipment, Plow & Hearth Catalog, Racedeck, Schulte Storage, and Sporty's Tool Shop.

Contents

Garage Solutions PROJECTS

Tool Hangers 20

Use your garage walls and a system of **MODULAR HANGERS** to organize your collection of home and garden tools

Sports Gear Locker 30

Got games? This multipurpose **SPORTS GEAR STORAGE STATION** stacks and racks whatever gets you going, no sweat

Entry Upgrade 42

Create a **GEAR ZONE** between your garage and house to contain a collection of clothing and equipment

Workshop Solutions 54

Transform a bare garage wall into a multipurpose **WORKSHOP AREA** featuring cabinets, work surface & electrical outlets

How to Use This Book

I F YOU'RE INTERESTED IN HOME IMPROVEMENTS that add value and convenience while also enabling you to express your own sense of style, you've come to the right place. **Do It Now/Do It Fast/Do It Right** books are created with an attitude that says "Let's get started!" and an ideal mix of home-improvement inspiration and how-to information. Do It Now books don't skip important steps or force you to guess at what needs to be done to take a project from start to finish.

You'll find that this book has a friendly, easy-to-use format. (See the sample pages shown here.) You'll begin each project knowing exactly what tools and gear you'll need, and what materials to buy at your home center or building-supply outlet. You can get started confidently because every step is illustrated and explained. Along the way, you'll discover plenty of expert advice packed into the margins. For ideas on how to personalize your project, check out the design options pages that follow the step-by-step instructions.

WORK TOGETHER

If you like company when you go to the movies or clean up the garage, you'll probably feel the same way about tackling home-improvement projects. The work will go faster, and you'll have a partner to share in the adventure. You'll

Get the **TOOLS & GEAR** you need. You'll also find out what features and details are important.

COOL TOOL guides you to the latest equipment to make tasks easy.

DO IT RIGHT tells you what it takes to get top-notch results.

WHAT TO BUY helps you put together your project shopping list, so you get all the materials you need.

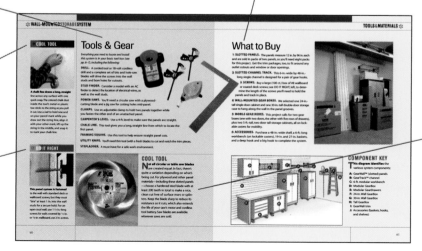

COOL TOOL puts you in touch with tools that make the job easier.

see that some projects really call for another set of hands to steady a ladder or keep the project going smoothly. Read through the project you'd like to tackle, and note where you're most likely to need help.

PLANNING AND PRACTICE PAY OFF

Most of the projects in this book can easily be completed in a weekend. But the job can take longer if you don't pay attention to planning and project-preparation requirements. Check out the conditions in the area where you'll be working in case repairs are required before you can begin your project. In the GET SET chapter (beginning on the next page), you'll find useful information on getting organized and on many of the tools, fasteners, and glue used in storage projects.

Your skill and confidence will improve with every project you complete. But if you're trying a technique for the first time, it's wise to rehearse before you "go live." This means ordering a little extra in the way of supplies and materials, and finding a location where you can practice your technique.

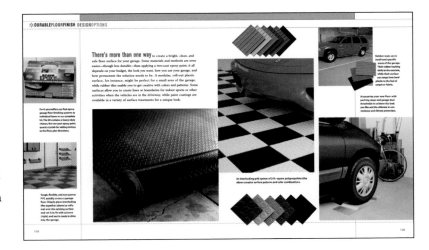

DESIGN OPTIONS Personalize your project with alternatives, finishes, add-ons, and details that suit your space and your sense of style.

WHAT CAN GO WRONG explains how to avoid common mistakes.

DO IT NOW helps to keep your project on track with timely advice.

STEP BY STEP Get started, keep going, and finish the job. Every step is illustrated and explained.

Get Set

With the right **TOOLS, GEAR & MATERIALS,** you can tackle any garage improvement project with confidence and ease

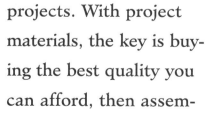

E MBARKING ON A GARAGE IMPROVEMENT is an exciting venture that will yield dramatic results and useful solutions. The first step—and arguably the most important—is to equip yourself with the tools, gear, and materials you'll need to be successful. You'll find that many of the basic tools needed for most home improvement projects will also serve you well for these garage projects. With project materials, the key is buying the best quality you can afford, then assembling and installing the projects carefully according to the instructions in this book.

✛ WHAT CAN GO WRONG

Most cordless drills are great for handling medium-duty jobs, but some lack the torque—turning power—to drive a heavy lag screw or similar fastener into a structural frame. If you invest in a cordless drill or screwdriver, get one with adequate torque and make sure its battery pack fits the other cordless tools you own or is part of a set.

▪ LINGO

For communication's sake think of bubble levels and carpenter's levels as synonymous; a torpedo level, however, is typically less than a foot long and may be tapered at the ends to help it fit into small spaces.

Basic Tool Box

Your project preparation begins with a basic toolset. Many tools serve multiple tasks for almost every home improvement job. While a few of these can be rented or borrowed from a friend, the bulk of them are simply good to keep around the house … er, garage.

DRILL. Go with a 1/3-horsepower or larger corded or cordless drill to deliver the power for almost any job yet still remain lightweight and easy to handle. Those with keyless chucks for fast bit changes are best.

DRILL BITS. Complete sets of drill bits and flat- and Phillips-head screwdriver heads are essential; you'll also need a 3/4-in. countersink bit to recess screws, a hole-saw bit, and a set of carbide-tipped or masonry bits for drilling tough materials such as concrete. Consider a set of socket bits to supplement a manual socket-wrench kit because it's often faster and easier to use.

STUD FINDER. This'll come in handy all over the house, but especially when you want to hang something heavy (like a heavy cabinet or load-bearing shelf) that requires structural support. Consider upgrading to a finder with a laser level for even more versatility with one tool.

CARPENTER'S PENCIL. Tougher than a #2 pencil from your child's school supplies, a flat carpenter's pencil not only stays put on your work surface, but also draws a sharp line and leaves a distinctive mark wherever needed. Add a sharpener designed for the pencil's special profile to make obtaining a fine point quick and easy.

HAND TOOLS. You'll also want a grip-molded utility knife and at least three extra blades, a pair of standard and needle-nose pliers, a 16-oz. hammer, a rubber mallet, a socket wrench set, a caulk gun, and a chalk line.

CLEANING TOOLS.
A clean workspace is essential, both before and after your garage improvement project. Use a heavy-duty whisk broom and dustpan to complement a stiff bristle push broom. Consider buying or renting a residential-scale power washer, and get a garden hose and multi-set nozzle— they'll all come in handy for many projects and chores.

STRAIGHTEDGE AND LEVELS. A 3-ft. straightedge will help you draw lines and make cuts accurately. Have a set of bubble levels, including a 4-ft., 2-ft., and torpedo styles—or perhaps a laser level—to ensure your shelves, cabinets, cleats, and other components are installed straight and stay that way.

MEASURING TAPE. A 25-ft. or 30-ft. retractable steel measuring tape gives you enough length to measure along a standard garage wall or ceiling.

SAW SET. A power saw does the job faster and cleaner than a hand saw. A corded or cordless circular saw makes quick work of most jobs. Also consider a table saw, a radial-arm saw, or a compound-miter saw, available at most home-improvement or hardware stores for purchase or rent.

STEP LADDER. A 6-ft. aluminum or a wooden step ladder will get you safely up to the ceiling or high up on a wall. Get one that has a shelf for holding tools, cans of paint, your various fasteners, and other gear within handy reach.

VOLTAGE TESTER. A good tool to have around the house, a voltage tester comes in handy if you add an extra electrical outlet or replace or add light fixtures in your garage. Most include a continuity tester for simple hot-wire checking. High-quality models have a variety of functions, including a polarity tester that makes sure that receptacles with polarized outlets are wired correctly for use with high-tech equipment.

▐▌ LINGO

A cleat is a small block of wood, usually of 2× material, bolted to the wall studs to support the weight of a bench or cabinet. The cleat adds rigidity to an open-backed storage unit or chest seat without the need to install a solid back.

✚ WHAT CAN GO WRONG

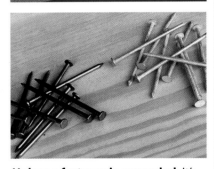

Unless a fastener is concealed, it's a good idea to use non-corrosive screws and nails on any building project—and it's especially true for those exposed to the elements, such as an outdoor shed or recycling center. Coated fasteners, including galvanized zinc (right), won't rust in humid or wet conditions, and they'll maintain their holding capacity.

Building Materials

Each project has a specific set of materials you'll need to complete the job, but here's a rundown of the staples you can expect to use on just about any garage improvement project.

2× LUMBER. Most often, you'll use 2×4 or 2×6 lumber to create a wood frame against a concrete wall or to cut and attach a cleat to hold the back of a storage bench or cabinet. Keep some scrap pieces around as filler or to help nudge a cabinet into place.

INSULATION. You'll need rolls of fiberglass batts (see specific projects for precise dimensions) or 4-ft. by 8-ft. panels of rigid foam insulation to fill the stud wall cavities and create a more comfortable and quiet garage work area.

WALLBOARD. Also called gypsum drywall, these 4-ft. by 8-ft. panels in $5/8$-in. thicknesses can be nailed or screwed to the wall studs, then finished for a clean, paintable wall with a surface that's smooth or textured.

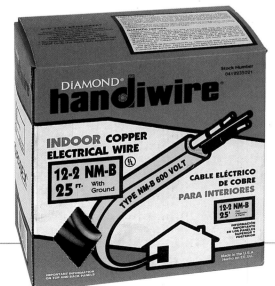

ELECTRICAL COMPONENTS. Romex® cable (220-rated 12-2 with ground, type NM-B), available in large rolls or by the foot, provides all the wires you need to extend an electrical outlet. You may also need a GFCI-equipped receptacle, plastic wire nuts, junction and outlet boxes with cable clamps, and electrical tape—all of which are applicable to a variety of household electrical jobs.

FASTENERS. Depending on the job, you may need lag screws; anchor sleeves, hollow-wall anchors, or toggle bolts (to secure to wallboard only); machine screws (for flush screw-head installations); and masonry nails or Tapcon®-type fasteners (which secure components to concrete or masonry blocks without epoxy or adhesives). Get corrosion-resistant screws for any outdoor projects that will be exposed to the elements. Most prepackaged storage units include the fasteners you'll need; some provide a drill, hex, or screw bit sized for the fasteners.

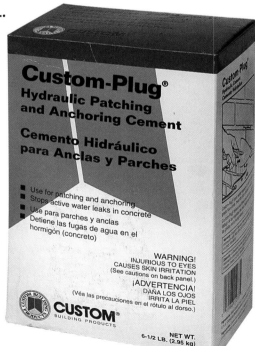

EXTERIOR-GRADE PLYWOOD. Also called T-111 siding, these 4-ft. by 8-ft. or larger sheets measure $3/8$ in. to $5/8$ in. thick and are either flat—"flush"—or embossed with a wood grain and/or a routed pattern on their exposed face.

READY-MIX CONCRETE AND PATCHING MATERIAL. Premixed bags of concrete and patching material mix with water for a fast and easy job; they also allow you to mix only what you need and save the rest for a future project. Make sure to follow mixing instructions to achieve the proper consistency and to ensure optimum curing or drying.

CABINETS AND CABINET MATERIALS. Make it easy on yourself with ready-to-assemble cabinets and other storage fixtures. For custom jobs, consider medium-density fiberboard (MDF) which cuts, works, and paints like solid wood but has less chance of splitting or warping.

CONSTRUCTION ADHESIVE. There are different products for different jobs, but they all do the same thing: glue one component (such as rigid-foam insulation panels) to another (such as a concrete wall). They eliminate the need for fasteners, ensure a reliable bond, and have great bonding strength. They are sold in tubes that fit standard caulking guns as well as in small tube-applicators.

⊘ UPGRADE

Closed-toe shoes are a must for proper safety, but steel-toe boots further improve your chances of avoiding injury. Sure, they're an investment, but a pair of high-quality leather boots will last a long time and might even save your toes along the way.

❖ COOL TOOL

If your garage storage project calls for lifting anything heavy—a cabinet or a shelf—or awkward—a sheet of wallboard—wear a light-weight support belt around your back and abdomen to help keep your spine aligned. Made from breathable, reinforced webbing for comfort and durability, the best ones feature multiple side pulls and suspenders for a snug fit.

Safety Gear

No job should be started without proper safety equipment. Depending on the project, you may be exposed to nasty fumes, saw and concrete dust, and flying shards of masonry or splinters of lumber. Avoid such hazards by using the following:

EYE PROTECTION. A good pair of safety goggles that wrap around your eyes and temples will protect your peepers from dust and debris. Make sure they fit comfortably—especially on the bridge of your nose and behind your ears—and use a strap to keep them snug against your head.

EAR PROTECTION. Power tools can generate noise levels equal to a jet engine at takeoff—or those of a heavy metal band. Wear earplugs or hearing protection whenever you perform noisy tasks.

WORK GLOVES. Medium-duty leather or nylon-and-leather work gloves are a must-have for almost any home improvement task. They provide comfort, protection, and flexibility. Make sure they fit your fingers—neither too long nor too short—and that their cuffs extend past your wrists to help keep sawdust, filings, and dirt from getting inside.

RUBBER AND LATEX GLOVES. For refinishing your garage floor and cleaning with strong detergents, you'll need a pair of heavy-duty rubber gloves—choose those that extend at least halfway up your forearms. Have an extra pair or two handy in case they rip or tear. Use latex gloves for fine work requiring dexterity.

FIRST-AID KIT. Every house and every garage should have its own kit, complete with compression and adhesive bandages, gauze, antiseptic wipes, small tubes of anti-bacterial and burn creams, small but sharp scissors, waterproof tape, and tweezers. A book of matches or a disposable lighter also comes in handy for sterilizing tools. Use hydrogen peroxide, applied with a cotton swab, to clean small wounds before you bandage them.

ALL PURPOSE FIRST AID
First Aid Kit
Recommended by Health Care Professionals
21 pieces
• Convenient size fits in luggage, briefcase, purse
• Be prepared away from home
FIRST AID ONLY. CONTENT FOR REAL LIFE

CLOSED-TOE SHOES. Protect your feet with a snug, comfortable pair of close-toe, lace-up shoes, preferably work boots or heavy-duty hiking boots. Your toes and the tops of your feet will thank you should a tool or piece of lumber fall from your workbench or stepladder.

DUST MASK. Protect your mouth and nose from dust, debris, and particles with disposable dust masks. Make sure the elastic band fits comfortably and holds the mask in place while you work.

PROPER-FITTING CLOTHES. Avoid loose-fitting clothing than might catch in moving tools, on protruding corners, or between materials while you work. Stick with jeans and T-shirts for woodworking, but always wear a long-sleeved work shirt when you use any cleaners and caustic chemicals, such as the muriatic-acid wash and epoxy paint needed for the garage floor refinishing project.

NUTRITION FIRST. Take periodic breaks when conditions are warm to keep yourself hydrated with water or sports drinks, and keep your energy level high with healthy snacks.

BACK IT UP. Take precautions when lifting anything—be it heavy, awkward, or when reaching overhead—to avoid a painful back, neck, or abdominal injury. Make sure to lift with your hips and legs—not your arms and back—and stand on a stable surface. Get help whenever you need to maneuver large or and cumbersome objects.

VENTILATION. No matter the garage improvement project, keep the garage door(s) open, as well as any auxiliary doors and windows to the outside, and consider using an oscillating electric fan when you paint, clean, or use solvents to bring in fresh air and exhaust fumes so that they dissipate quickly. Never work in a closed space with materials that emit explosive or toxic vapors.

Prep Projects

Whatever project you choose, PREPARING THE WALLS will make building and installing a garage storage solution faster and easier

E VERY HOME IMPROVEMENT PROJECT REQUIRES PREPARATION, and building and installing new garage storage systems are no exception. For a more comfortable and quieter garage, you'll want to insulate the walls using either fiberglass rolls or rigid foam insulation panels. To distribute more electrical power around the garage, consider extending your existing service with an extra outlet or two. And if you're going to hang anything on the walls or ceiling—be it a heavy-duty shelf, a storage cabinet, or a bike rack—you'll need to find the structural frame and use the proper fasteners to ensure it stays in place.

INSULATE   ADD AN OUTLET   FIND THE FRAMING   FASTEN A STORAGE UNIT

▸ LINGO

All insulating material has an R-value, a rating measure of its resistance to heat flow at a certain thickness. The higher the R-value, the better the insulating performance of the material.

∴ DO IT FAST

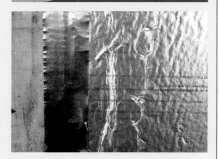

If you don't want to mess with construction adhesive and a caulking gun to fasten the rigid foam panels, you can opt for foil joint tape that seals joints between panels and fastens the panels to the framing, sealing out air leaks. After the panels are in place, run tape their full length at each joint and where they meet the studs. When you apply wallboard or paneling as a finishing step, the foam panels will be sealed behind it.

Insulate with Rolls

1 **ROLL IT OUT.** Choose insulation with the same widths and thicknesses as are found in your wall cavities between studs (typically 3½ in. deep for a 2 × 4 wall). Wear gloves and a dust mask. Start at the top of the wall, unrolling the insulation with its Kraft-paper side facing out, and filling the cavity completely without compressing the insulation. Unfold the Kraft-paper flaps as you go, stapling them to the studs every 12 in. Cut the roll to length at the bottom with a utility knife.

2 **CUT AROUND INTRUSIONS.** Use a utility knife to cut the insulation to fit it around and sandwich any pipes or electrical wires running through the wall studs. To preserve the insulation's R-value (see LINGO, left), avoid compressing or forcing it around intrusions or junction boxes. To work around particularly complex intrusions, cut the roll into smaller sections and overlap the paper backing when you hang it.

Insulate with Foam Panels

1 **FRAME THE WALL.** To create a stud wall cavity on a concrete wall, first measure the wall's height and use a circular saw to cut 2 × 4 studs that length. Space studs 16 in. apart, measuring between the centers of each pair of studs. Fasten each stud's wide face to the the concrete wall with fluted masonry nails or Tapcon® screws, making a 1½-in.-deep cavity.

2 **FASTEN THE PANELS.** Measure the height and width of each cavity. Cut 1½-in.-thick rigid foam insulation panels with a utility knife and a straightedge to fit each cavity. Cut or notch the panels to fit around obstructions or to fill areas with odd dimensions. Apply construction adhesive  to the concrete wall, press the panel firmly into the cavity, and hold it in place for a few minutes until the adhesive bonds the panel to the wall surface.

Electrical circuit capacity is expressed in amps, the amount of electrical current a circuit can carry along its wires. Most circuits have the capacity to accommodate a few outlets.

◆ DO IT NOW

How do you add outlets on a concrete wall? Simply attach a so-called outlet strip of prewired electrical outlets. Make sure that the circuit powering the nearest junction box has enough amperage capacity to handle the outlets on the strip, then connect the wires at one end of the outlet strip to the junction box.

❖ COOL TOOL

A voltage tester comes in handy whether you're adding an outlet, determining the amperage capacity of a circuit, or trying to find the precise location of an electrical outage or other problem. It's also safer and more convenient to use than plugging an appliance or tool into an outlet to see if it has power.

Add an Electrical Outlet

1 **FIND THE SOURCE.** Find the wall stud you want to mount your new outlet on, and locate the nearest existing outlet from which you'll extend the power. Ideally, use the last outlet in the chain (or "run") from the service panel so you don't have to connect two sets of wires; it'll be the one farthest away from the panel. Shut off the power to that run at the panel—confirm it with a voltage tester—and remove the outlet's faceplate. Next, unscrew and remove the outlet from the box to gain access to its wires and the terminal clamps behind it. Measure the distance to the new outlet and cut Romex® cable to that length *plus* an extra 12 in. for slack.

2 **DRILL THE STUDS.** Use a carpenter's level and pencil to mark a straight line from the existing outlet to the new outlet location on the exposed wall studs. On those marks, bore a ¾-in. hole through the center of each stud along the line. Fasten steel guard plates on the outside narrow face of the studs, over the holes, to protect the wires running through the studs from wallboard nails or screws.

3 **CONNECT THE WIRES.** Fasten the outlet box flush with the wall studs plus the thickness of the wallboard. Run the end of the cable from any keyhole in the box, clamping the cable with box clamps and stapling it to the studs along vertical runs. Insert the cable into the existing outlet, leaving some slack, and clamp it in place. At each end, strip back 6 in. of the sheathing to reveal the cable wires; separate the wires, and strip their insulation ⅜ in. from their ends. Connect the black-sheathed wire to a brass outlet clamp and the white-sheathed wire to a silver clamp. Wrap the green grounding wire around the screws in the back of each outlet box.

4 **TEST AND FINISH.** Turn on power to the circuit and use a voltage tester to check that both outlets are receiving power (typically 115 volts). Turn off the power, fasten the receptacles to their respective outlet boxes, then attach their faceplates with screws.

1

2

3

4

✓ UPGRADE

Consider the multiple benefits of a stud finder–laser level tool, which not only locates framing members, but also casts a straight and level beam of light. Some laser levels also send beams in more than one direction simultaneously and can be tilted for angled placements.

▶ DO IT RIGHT

Why drill pilot holes? Any intrusion—especially a screw fastener—can split the face of a wall stud, greatly reducing its ability to hold the fastener (and thus your shelf or cabinet) tightly to the wall. Prevent splits and create some space by predrilling a hole about ⅛ in. in diameter smaller than the diameter of the screw to be installed.

✛ SAFETY FIRST

To support heavyweight shelves and racks from wallboard alone use a toggle bolt with spring-loaded wings instead of a hollow-wall anchor. It can support a greater load by grasping a larger area of wallboard.

Fasten Items to a Wall

1 **FIND THE FRAMING.** If wallboard or paneling covers the frame members, use a stud finder to locate them. Mark the location of each stud with a pencil, then use a level to draw a line along its vertical length.

2 **FASTEN WITH LAG SCREWS.** Whatever you're fastening to a framing member, such as a wall stud, a lag screw is the best choice to hold it in place and to support its weight. Position the unit on the wall—a cabinet, shelf, or rack—and mark each screw's location on the unit's back panel by transferring the line from step 1, above. Drill a pilot hole through the unit into the center of the frame member behind it, "grease" the screw's threads with soap or graphite to reduce friction, then use a socket wrench to tighten the lag screw.

3 **USE HOLLOW-WALL ANCHORS.** While you should always attach at least one fastener to a frame member, it may be necessary to secure the other end of a long, lightweight storage unit through the wallboard between framing members and still give it adequate support. Drill a hole in the wallboard just large enough to accept a hollow-wall anchor, unscrew the bolt from the anchor's sleeve, thread it onto the storage unit, and rethread the bolt into the sleeve. Insert the hollow-wall anchor into the hole in the wallboard, then tighten its bolt. The anchor's outer sleeve will compress behind the wallboard as you tighten it, grasping the wallboard.

4 **ATTACH TO CONCRETE.** Concrete walls are structural and they can carry the added weight of shelves, cabinets, or racks. To ensure a secure hold, mark and drill pilot holes for Tapcon® screws that are at least ¼ in. deeper than the length of the screws, using 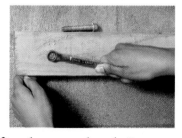 the bit provided with the fasteners or one that fits the screwhead. Screw-fasten your storage unit, cleat, or ledger board to the wall, taking care not to over-tighten the fasteners in the pilot holes—it can cause their heads to snap off.

1

2

3

4

Tool Hangers

Use your garage walls and a system of **MODULAR HANGERS** to organize your collection of home and garage tools

W OULDN'T IT BE NICE TO HAVE ONE PLACE IN THE GARAGE where all of your yard and garden tools, coils of rope, hoses, car-washing gear, and small hand tools were conveniently stored *and* accessible? With some simple, wall-mounted fixtures and a grid system with your choice of hooks, baskets, and shelves, you can quickly and easily create that storage spot. All you need is a few basic tools and a few hours; then you'll be ready to start hanging your tools. This modular system is also easy to adapt and redesign to accommodate new tools as your collection and needs grow.

LOCATE THE SPACE   **FASTEN THE RACK**   **ADD HOOKS AND HANGERS** **ATTACH ACCESSORIES**

✦ DO IT NOW

While a modular system is flexible, take stock of what you need before you go out and buy your fixtures and hooks. Determine which tools and other gear you'll hang—even how best to store them—to create a shopping list of hooks, baskets, and shelves.

✱ WHAT'S DIFFERENT?

Like the slatwall system shown on p. 78, this modular grid system helps you customize your storage along your garage walls. But this grid's woven design delivers a more "open" appearance and weighs less. Beware: it doesn't support heavy cabinets or work surfaces.

Tools & Gear

Everything you need to locate and install this system is in your basic tool box (see pp. 6–7), including the following:

DRILL. Leverage the power and torque provided by a corded tool or an 18-volt cordless drill to drive the mounting fasteners into the wall studs.

STUD FINDER. A battery-powered stud finder locates the wall framing members behind wallboard or paneling, and it reveals the distance between wall studs.

CARPENTER'S LEVEL. Use a 4-ft. level to make sure your grid panels are straight before you fasten them to the wall.

TAPE MEASURE AND PENCIL. You'll need these to determine your overall surface area and to mark the location of the wall studs and mounting hardware. Keep a sharp tip on a flat carpenter's pencil with a special sharpener designed for this type of pencil (see COOL TOOL, below).

STEPLADDER. You may need one or two, depending on your layout: the first is for yourself and the other other is for a helper if the grid panel is fastened high on the wall.

COOL TOOL

A special sharpener for a carpenter's pencil may not be a necessity, but it's safer, faster, and more reliable than using a utility or pocket knife for keeping a fine point at the ready. About the size of a pack of gum (or even smaller), it fits easily into your nail bag or utility belt; in a few quick strokes, it delivers a flat point that marks cleanly and lasts longer than any point you can carve with a knife.

What to Buy

1| WALL-MOUNTED GRID PANEL.
Available in 2-ft. by 4-ft. sections with six mounting brackets per section, the grid panel can be used alone or in combination with additional grids to accommodate your storage needs. All fasteners and hardware should come in the package.

2| ACCESSORIES AND FIXTURES.
Most grid panel systems offer a wide range of accessories, from those that hang on the grid panel to wall-mounted hooks, baskets, and shelves that add permanent functionality to your storage system. Consider other hanging fixtures that suit special tools such as lawn rakes and string trimmers for weeds.

RIGHT-SIZED SYSTEM

As you plan where to put your grid panel, be sure to consider the length and shape of your yard and garden tools and other gear. While long-handled tools can hang below the bottom edge of the grid panel, you'll need to place the panel high enough on the wall to leave enough clearance for them; the same rule applies to wide, horizontally stored items, such as extension ladders, that require several feet along the face of the wall. Tip: Lay out the grid panel and tools on the floor or your driveway before you install any of the panel's hardware.

:: **LINGO**

Wallboard is the common name for gypsum drywall, which is a covering usually installed over the wall stud framing inside houses and garages to finish their walls, concealing the insulation, wires, and pipes that run between and through their framing.

◑ **NEED A HAND?**

While the 2-ft. by 4-ft. open-wire grid panel is lightweight and can be handled on your own, trying to hold it in place with one hand as you manipulate a level, tape measure, pencil, and drill is a recipe for a crooked grid panel. Temporarily fasten one of the panel's top corners in place with a wood screw while you level and fasten its other corners. With them in place, replace the wood screw with a permanent fastener.

Create a Complete System

1 **CHOOSE THE PLACE.** Depending on the tools you want to hang and your shopping list, (see pp. 22–23), find an area on an interior garage wall with ample space to install the system. Using your stud finder, mark the location and spacing of the wall studs behind the wallboard; the spacing between the studs will be either 16 in. or 24 in. apart. Use your level and pencil to draw a straight line down the center of each stud. With your tape measure and pencil, locate and mark the height of the top of the grid panel or panels on the wall.

2 **LOCATE THE PANEL.** Position a grid panel with its top edge flush to the mark you just made. Hold it in place with a temporary wood screw (see NEED A HAND?, left), and adjust it as you check that it is level and plumb (vertically straight). Mark a precise line both  vertically and horizontally so the grid panel won't slip out of level as you fasten it. Hold the grid panel tight to the reference lines as you adjust each mounting bracket into position over a wall stud.

3 **FASTEN THE GRID.** With the grid panel held firmly in place, drill a pilot hole through each mounting bracket's holes, through the wallboard beneath, and into the wall stud. Screw the brackets to the wall using the fasteners provided in the unit's package. Work across the top of the panel first, checking to make sure it stays level and plumb as you work, then mount the brackets along the bottom. Remove the screw and attach the last bracket.

4 **ADD ACCESSORIES.** Attach your choice of accessories to the grid panel—they require no fasteners, but must mount properly— and fasten other fixed hooks or shelves directly to the wall studs outside the grid panel, following your layout plan. Now, hang your tools and gear.

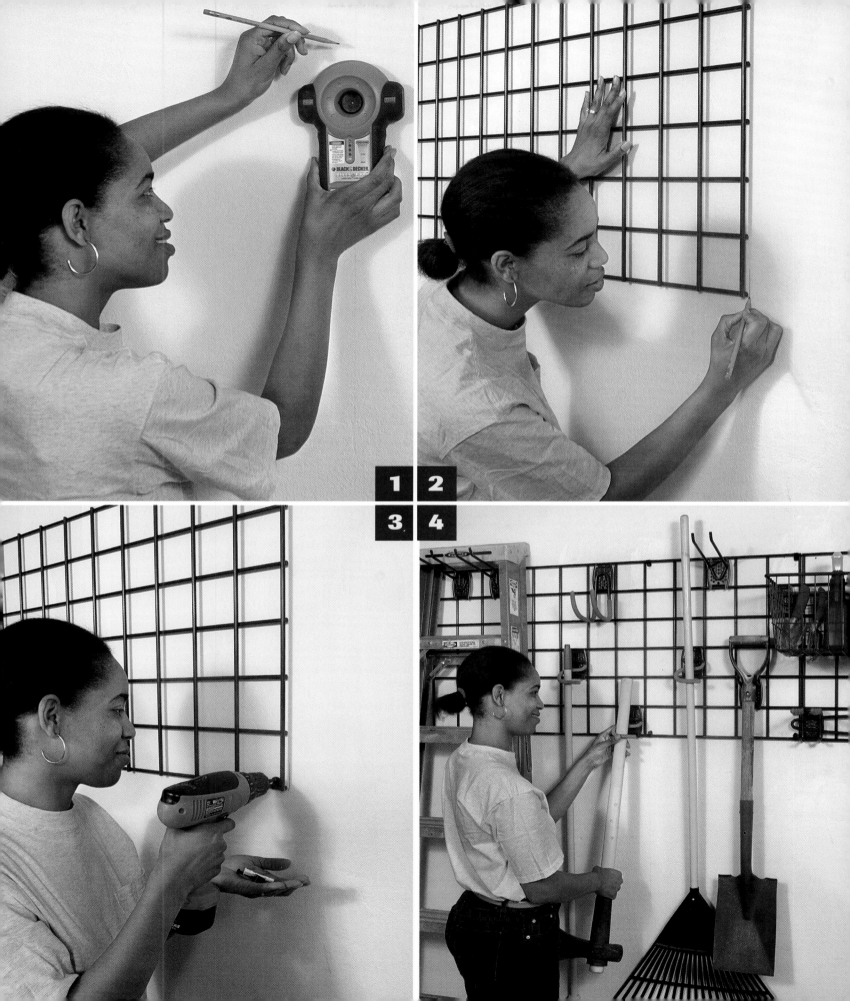

A wall-hung storage solution affords you maximum flexibility to create a space-efficient, convenient place for a wide variety of yard and garden tools, containers, ropes, sports equipment…really, anything you need to keep handy but also neatly out of the way. Mount hooks, baskets, shelves, and other accessories on either the grid panel or the adjacent wall. Get creative with shelves and hooks; even the most simple types can boost your garage's storage capacity. Just be sure they're fastened to the wall safely and securely.

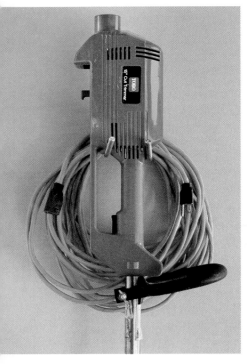

Special brackets support heavy, awkward equipment such as weed trimmers, leaf blowers, and pruning poles. They have long arms that grasp and secure the tool and its power cord.

Deep-throated hooks enable you to hang coils of hose and electrical cords. They can also support stepladders, which have rungs that fit nicely into the hook's open jaw.

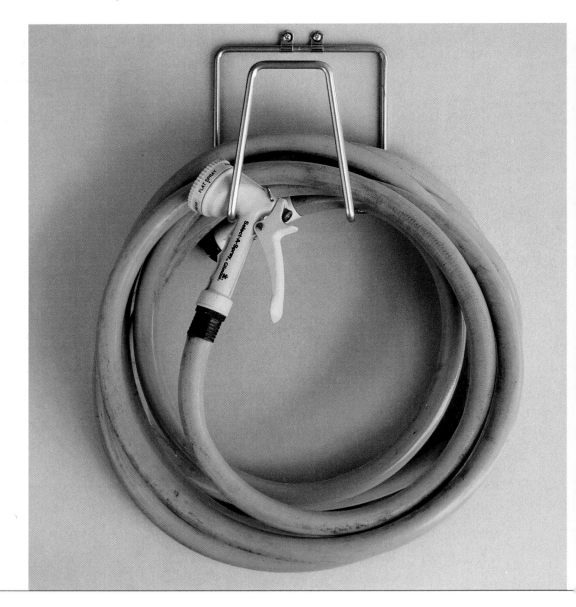

Combination hangers have shelves, deep-throated hooks, and detachable carrier baskets that can be loaded with tools for storage, yet lift off for transport to your job location. Even though they are sold for use with garden tools, they work equally well with carpentry, woodworking, and machine shop tools.

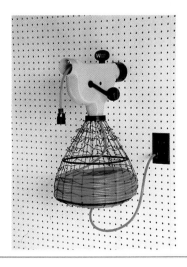

A swivel bracket and a cord winder makes short work of a perennially difficult storage challenge. Just pull out the cord when needed, then reel it back into the hanging basket when the job is done.

Use a loop hook to keep hoses, extension cords, and ropes coiled and ready when not in use. Roll up the cord or hose first, then latch the hook around the coil and hang it on a wall hook.

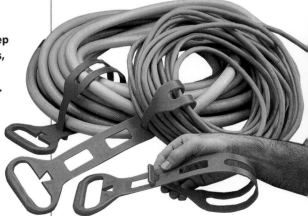

Store an extension or stepladder using two heavy-duty hooks on a grid or slatwall system, or mount them directly to the wall frame. Hang ladders at chest height or lower so that they're easy to take down when you want to use them and are quickly stored when you're finished.

Consider using a combination hook that attaches to a permanently installed mount fastened to the garage's frame members. Place a mount at several locations; that way the hooks can be relocated as often and easily as your need for tools changes.

Some systems sell accessories in a convenient pack, including a variety of hooks, shelves, and baskets; individual accessories sold separately supplement these packaged kits.

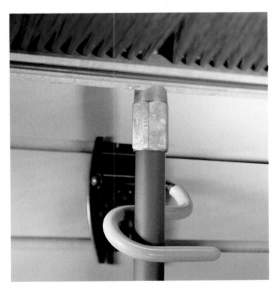 

A hinged hook (left) grips a broom, mop, or rake handle at any point along its length, allowing it to lay flat against the wall when not in use. A multipurpose hook (right) offers maximum storage flexibility and is strong enough to carry the weight of a power hedge trimmer, leaf blower, bike, or carpentry tool.

Sports Gear Locker

Got games? This multipurpose SPORTS GEAR STORAGE STATION stacks and racks whatever gets you going, no sweat

TODAY'S SPORTS LANDSCAPE IS BURSTING WITH VARIETY, and chances are good that your collection of athletic gear has followed suit—most of it scattered somewhere in your garage. From bikes to boards, basketballs to bocce-ball sets, and tennis rackets to golf bags, sports equipment takes on lots of shapes and sizes…and takes up precious garage space. Help is on the way with this multifunctional cabinet and racking system that's easy to assemble. It consolidates, organizes, and shelters your gear in a compact space. You'll not only open up your garage for other uses, but you'll also have a dedicated area where you can always find whatever you need—no matter your game.

ASSEMBLE CABINETS   **BUILD A CHEST**   **ADD ACCESSORIES**   **ADD RACKS AND FILL**

✓ **UPGRADE**

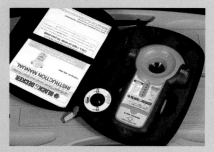

A stud finder combined with a laser level is a great addition to your all-purpose tool box. The beam of the laser level is a hands-free way to check whether cabinets, racking systems, or other wall-hung components are straight before you fasten them to the wall's framing members.

LINGO

Many cabinets—including the one shown here—are built in frame-and-panel style. The frame members along the outside edges are either vertical stiles or horizontal rails; a panel attached across the back and sides encloses the frame.

Tools & Gear

Make sure you have the following tools close at hand and your cordless batteries are charged up before you get into the game.

CORDED OR CORDLESS DRILL. A keyless chuck (see COOL TOOL, below) makes changing from drill bits to screw bits fast and easy, while the extra power from a corded tool or 18-volt cordless motor helps drive fasteners into the framing members.

STUD FINDER. A battery-powered stud finder—or stud sensor—makes locating the framing members (wall studs) a breeze and much more precise.

RUBBER MALLET. The broad and buffeted force of this tool allows you to assemble the cabinets and storage chest and nudge them into place without damaging their factory finishes.

CARPENTER'S LEVEL. Use this tool to make sure the cabinets and racking systems hang straight and plumb on the wall.

SOCKET WRENCH SET. This will come in handy for tightening the lag screws you'll use to fasten the cabinets and chest to the wall. Or get a set of sockets for your corded drill to boost the torque and speed the installation.

COOL TOOL

If you've ever lost or stripped a chuck key as you swap out drill and screw bits on an old corded drill/driver, consider retrofitting that tool with a keyless chuck. Not only does it save the hassle of using (or perhaps finding) your chuck key, but it grips bits tightly to ensure they stay put as you work. The accessory installs on most ³⁄₈-in. drills in mere minutes with a hex wrench, and it provides comfortable molded grips to protect your hands.

What to Buy

1| PREFINISHED CABINETS. A pair of 60-in.- to 72-in.-tall by 24-in.-wide cabinets, packaged with all the frame-and-panel components, fasteners, and hardware (plus step-by-step assembly instructions), provides the space you need to conceal, protect, and store seasonal sports gear.

2| PREFINISHED STORAGE CHEST. Like the cabinets, this handy and extensive floor chest is packaged with its hardware and prefinished for easy and fast assembly. It's the perfect place for athletic gear such as shoes, cleats, boots, fins, spikes, skates, blades, helmets, and protective pads.

3| RACKING SYSTEMS. The choice of modular components is yours, depending on the games you play. This project uses a specialized shelf system set between two tall cabinets to hold balls of various sizes, gloves, and shoes. Buy smaller, specialty rack-and-shelf systems to outfit the cabinets inside and out to hang gear such as skis, poles, and golf bags.

4| SHIMS. Buy a set of composite wood shims (instead of flimsy wood shims) to place under the cabinets and chest, as necessary, so the assembled components sit level and firm on the garage floor.

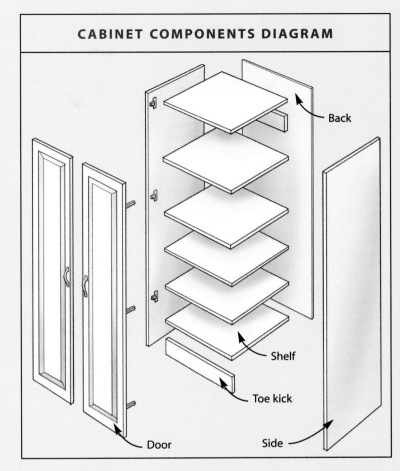

CABINET COMPONENTS DIAGRAM

Back

Shelf

Toe kick

Door

Side

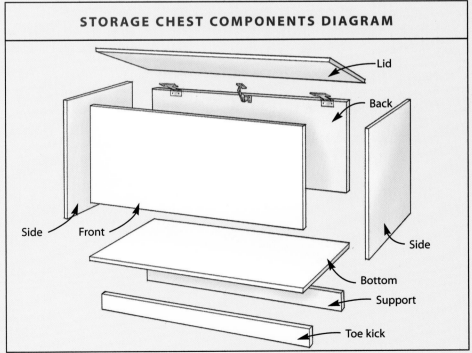

STORAGE CHEST COMPONENTS DIAGRAM

Lid

Back

Side

Side

Front

Bottom

Support

Toe kick

◑ NEED A HAND?

It typically takes two people to properly set a 6-ft.-tall by 2-ft.-wide cabinet in place without damaging its edges or factory finish. Wait until the cabinets are in place to attach their doors, but rely on a helper and maybe even a small hand truck to easily move the unit into place and carefully set it against the wall.

╋ WHAT CAN GO WRONG

Despite the best measuring, slight miscalculations can cause you to reset a cabinet. Install only one of the tall side cabinets before placing the chest and racking system between them. This will potentially save time and lower the risk of damaging its back panel.

Build & Install the Cabinet

1 **FIND A LOCATION.** You need a clear wall space of at least 6½ ft. across, 6 ft. tall, and 24 in. to 30 in. deep to accommodate the cabinets, chest, and racks. Make sure you'll have enough clearance to fully open the cabinet doors with a parked vehicle nearby. With a pencil, mark off the area and locate each wall stud; use a level and a pencil to mark the length of each stud for reference. Assemble your cabinets and chest nearby to make them easier to move into place against the wall.

2 **ASSEMBLE THE CABINETS.** Using the hardware and fasteners provided with the cabinets, follow the instructions to assemble the units. Leave the doors off until the cabinets are fastened to the wall. Set the assembled cabinets loosely in place according to your previously drawn marks and transfer the stud locations to the inside face of each cabinet's back panel. Shim the cabinets' bottoms, if necessary, so they stand level and plumb against the wall and are stable on the floor.

3 **ATTACH THE CABINETS.** Install the first cabinet, leaving the second until after you fasten the chest and racking system into place. Drill pilot holes through the unit's back panel every 18 in. down the length of the wall studs, using a drill bit slightly smaller than the

lag screws—hold them side by side for comparison. Check for level again, adjust the shims as needed, and fasten the cabinet to the wall with 2-in. to 3-in. lag screws—or those provided with the cabinet. Tighten the screws with a socket wrench or with a socket mounted on your drill.

4 **OUTFIT THE CABINETS.** Add hangers and small specialty racks inside the cabinet to accommodate various sports equipment, or install hooks to hold canvas or mesh bags for balls and gear. Hang premade ski-and-snowboard or bicycle hangers on the outside face of the cabinet if you have adequate clearance beyond the cabinet space.

▶ DO IT RIGHT

It's easy to overtighten lag screws in a wall stud. If you see the back panel of the chest or cabinet start to pull toward the wall or the pressed wood compress, reverse the turn of your socket or other wrench and back out the screw until it is flush with the panel surface and the warp is gone. Don't worry; there's still plenty of screw in the stud to properly support the chest.

◼ LINGO

A tool's **torque** refers to its turning or twisting force, specifically the power it delivers to rotate a screw, bolt, or drill bit into a wall stud or ceiling joist; the more torque a tool has, the easier it is to drive the fastener or drill bit.

Add a Chest

5 **ASSEMBLE THE CHEST.** Using the hardware and fasteners packaged with the chest components, follow the manufacturer's instructions to assemble the storage chest. Protect the unit's finished edges and panels by using a rubber mallet to coax the frame components together.

6 **SET IN PLACE.** Carefully transfer the assembled chest from your work area to its final location on the wall, flush against the tall cabinet already installed. Use your level to make sure the chest is level across the top and plumb on its sides; shim the bottom,  if necessary, to set it squarely in place in preparation for drilling holes to fasten it to the wall with lag screws.

7 **SECURE THE CHEST.** There will be at least one but likely two wall studs upon which to fasten—or hang—the chest to the wall. Using the same technique as for step 3 on p. 34, drill pilot holes through the back panel of the chest every 18 in. down the length of each stud. Check and adjust for level as needed, then fasten the unit to the wall with 2-in. to 3-in. lag screws. Tighten the screws with a socket wrench.

8 **FILL IT UP.** The storage chest is 15½ in. deep by 31¾ in. wide by 19½ in. tall, so it can handle lots of loose gear for just about every athletic endeavor. As options, add dividers to separate the equipment used for different sports or place the gear in bright-colored duffel 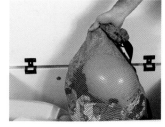 bags for easy access. The hinged lid will keep household dirt and debris to a minimum—provided you clean your footwear before stowing it—but avoid using the bench as a seat unless the manufacturer says that its top and hinges are strong enough to carry an adult's body weight.

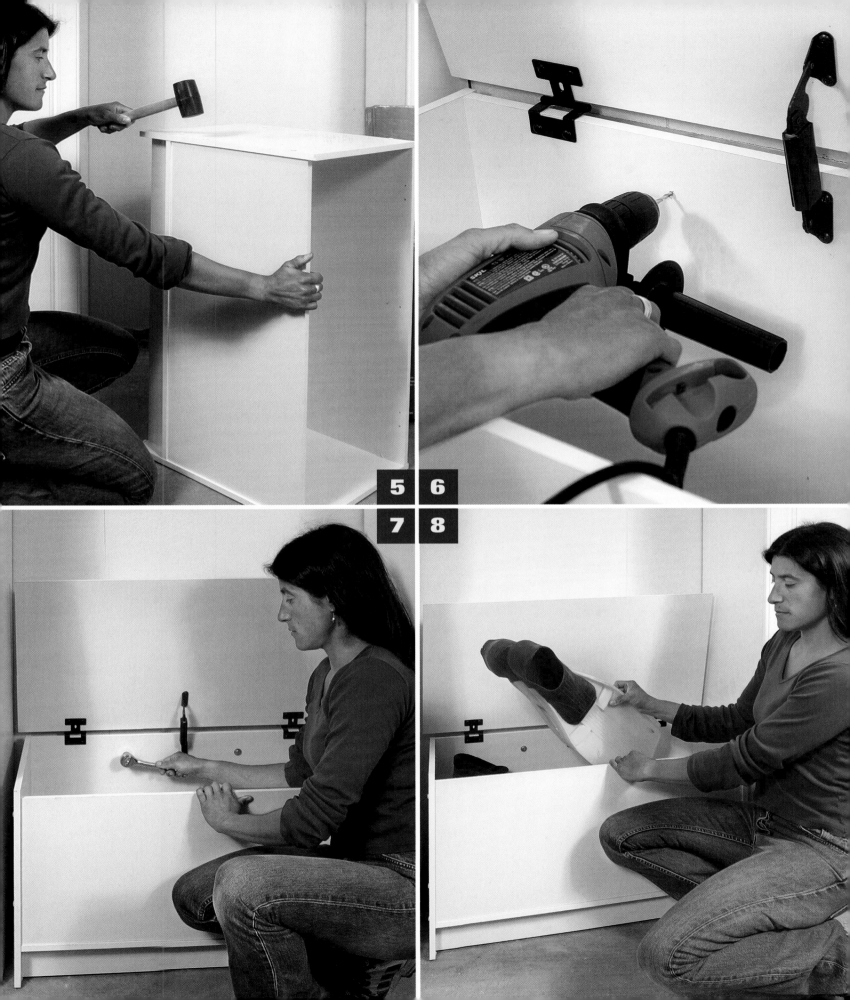

5 6
7 8

◆ DO IT NOW

If you use anchor sleeves to secure a slatwall panel or an open-rack pegboard panel to the wallboard, install them before you bolt the other end of the panel to the wall studs. You'll need the flexibility an open end gives to insert the sleeve through the wallboard and into the wall cavity.

UPGRADE

With a slatwall racking system, you can easily and quickly swap out the racks to accommodate new and different storage needs as your athletic interests evolve. Most systems offer an abundance of choices that can be mixed and matched for your gear.

Add Rack Systems

9 **CHECK STUD LOCATIONS.** Use the markings you made in Step 1 on p. 34 and the heads of the lag screws in the chest to locate the wall studs; in any 32-in. span, there should be two wall studs available. You can either attach both ends of the 33½-in.-wide by 28-in.-high racking system to the studs or fasten one end to a stud with lag screws and support the other end by fastening it to the wallboard alone using a hollow-wall anchor (see Step 3, p. 18). With the rack system in position, use a pencil to mark the location of each of its mounting holes.

10 **DRILL MOUNTING HOLES.** Prepare the rack system for installation to the wall by boring 5/32-in. pilot holes at each of the marked locations. They should bore into the studs or, if no stud exists, through the wallboard so that you can install anchor sleeves, hollow wall anchors, or toggle bolts.

11 **INSTALL THE RACK.** Set the rack system in position, check and adjust it for level and plumb, and fasten it in place with 2-in. to 3-in. lag screws into either solid wood or anchors into wallboard, or install and tighten the supplied screws or bolts. Slide the remaining tall cabinet into place flush and plumb with the chest and rack system, and secure it to the wall as you did in Step 3, p. 34. Hang the doors on both cabinets. Add interior and exterior racking systems, as desired; see Step 4, p. 34.

12 **STOW YOUR GEAR.** Adjust the hooks, racks, and shelves on the rack system to accommodate your needs, make the most use of the system, and create the display you want. Fill the rack system, cabinets, and chest with your various sports gear. Store equipment you use most often in the exposed racks between the cabinets and above the chest. Place fragile, seasonal, or occasionally used gear inside the cabinets or on hangers mounted to their outer walls. Use net bags to hang balls for soccer, basketball, and the like.

9 **10**

11 **12**

A multipurpose racking system that stores like-sized sports balls, racquets, skateboards, and other odd-shaped gear is perfect for a family of sports enthusiasts.

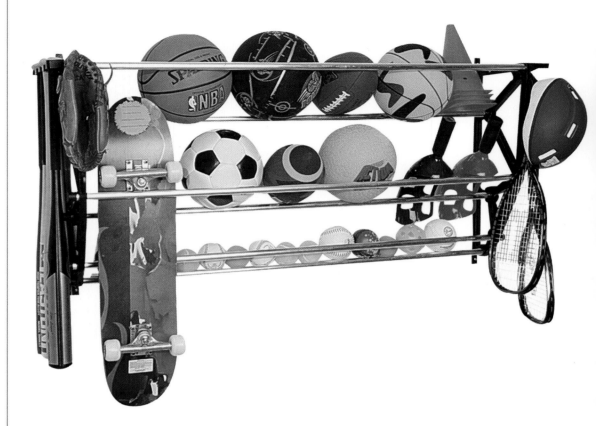

Sharp-edged downhill skis are a hazard if they're not stored securely. This rack keeps them in their place while also allowing you to stow your boots upright to save garage floor space.

A metal-framed sports bench with ventilated wire sides makes a good seat to use while you remove your shoes and a convenient spot to store damp gear until it dries.

There hasn't been a game invented that doesn't have some sort of gear or equipment that is best stored securely, safely, and conveniently for the next time you're ready to strap it on. So rest easy—there's a storage solution for gear used in both common and the most extreme sports that will fit somewhere in your garage, whether that spot is hanging against a wall, resting on the floor, or dangling overhead…or maybe a combination of all three.

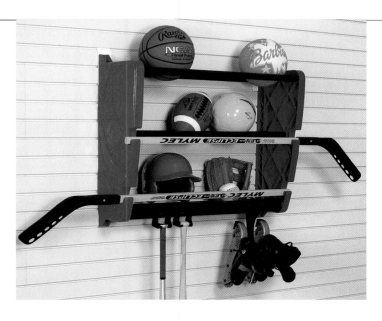

If a rollerblading fad has evolved into a street hockey passion, this rack system will stow your blades, sticks, pucks, and helmets in a convenient and compact area along with gear from other sports, including baseball, football, and soccer.

A pair of waist-high hangers is the right choice for hanging bicycles on the wall. To use the bike, just lift up and set the bike on its wheels—you'll be ready to break away in seconds.

Specialty hangers (above) make storing tennis, squash, racketball, and other racket sports equipment a snap. Use general hangers such as baskets and long hooks (left) to store ice skates, hockey helmets, and pads.

Entry Upgrade

Create a **GEAR ZONE** between your garage and house to contain a collection of clothing and equipment

THE MUD ROOM BY DEFAULT—that corner of the garage that leads into the house—is likely filled with an ever-growing collection of stuff you don't want to bring into your home. Here's a great way to organize the space so that it's useful and looks good too. Built from tough, good-looking materials, this multipurpose unit features a bench, hangers, and cubbies—perfect for keeping all of your outdoor gear close at hand and providing a place to sit and take off muddy boots. It's a weekend project that's easy and fun…and it will make a big difference to your home and garage.

BUILD A BENCH   **CONSTRUCT THE CUBBY**   **ATTACH A RACK**   **HOOK 'EM**

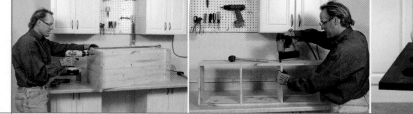

Tools & Gear

● NEED A HAND?

If you're a little anxious about using power tools, sign up for a class at your nearest home improvement store or through an adult education program at a local high school. Heck, a dealer might even give you a private lesson if you plan to buy the tools you need. Even after the class, practice with each tool on some scrap lumber until you're comfortable using your tools on the project materials.

◆ COOL TOOL

A router guide ensures accurate cuts. Simply clamp a straightedge on your material or use the finished edge of a scrap piece of plywood as a guide. With the router unplugged, measure from the bit to your pencil marks to set the cut to the guide and adjust the guide's location as necessary. Then follow the guide's edge with your router.

This is a tool-intensive project, but there's no need to buy everything. Consider renting the tools you need or borrowing them from a friend.

CARPENTRY TOOLS. You'll need a tape measure, carpenter's pencil, framing square, several clamps, block sander, 12-oz. finish hammer, rubber mallet, 4-ft. carpenter's level, socket set, putty knife, construction glue, and paintable wood paste.

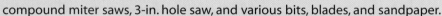

POWER TOOLS. In addition to a corded or cordless drill, you'll need a router, power belt and palm sander, brad nailer, circular and compound miter saws, 3-in. hole saw, and various bits, blades, and sandpaper.

SAWHORSES. Get your materials off the ground—and give your back and knees a break—with a pair of stable sawhorses or a portable workbench with adjustable clamps.

SAFETY GEAR. Whenever you saw or sand, make sure to wear safety glasses and a dust mask to protect your eyes and lungs. Avoid loose clothing, too.

PAINT BRUSHES. Have a set of 1½-in.- to 3-in.-wide brushes to apply the paint, stain, or varnish coats. Keeps some clean, lint-free rags handy, too, to wipe up drips and splatters.

COOL TOOL

Get off the floor and away from rickety sawhorses with the latest in portable elevated workbenches. Not only do they fold flat in seconds for compact storage, but they offer lockable wheels for mobility, anti-slip feet, and vises and clamps to hold your materials in place while you work; their tough steel construction can withstand lots of use and abuse. Adjustable to about 30 in. off the ground, they provide a stable, elevated work platform that eases stress on your back, legs, and knees.

What to Buy

1| PLYWOOD. Pine-based interior-grade plywood is a workable material for a project like this, and it delivers an attractive grain if you decide to stain the finished pieces. You'll need enough $1\frac{1}{8}$-in.- and $\frac{5}{8}$-in.-thick material to satisfy the lumber list (see LUMBER LIST, below), though you may be able buy the pieces precut or in smaller dimensions for quicker preparation and easier transport.

2| FASTENERS. Buy a half-dozen 2-in. lag screws to fasten the backboard to the wall, a dozen #6 round-head screws for the brackets and hinges, and a box of $1\frac{1}{2}$-in. flathead wood screws to fasten the panels.

3| HOOKS. The hardware style is up to you, but a double-hook design does twice the work in the same space.

4| STAIN OR PAINT. Select a desirable stain, varnish, or latex paint color, and make sure to keep mineral spirits on hand for easy clean-up. If you stain the wood, protect it with at least two layers of a polyurethane sealer.

5| HINGES. Buy a set of two weight-rated hinges and a 3-ft. piano hinge. Together, they keep the back of the boot bench lid from slamming shut. Most have spring-tension controls to adjust the angle of the opening and the amount of weight needed to close the lid.

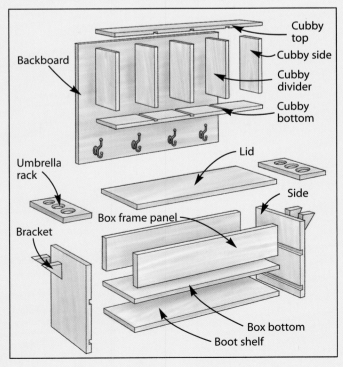

Whether you cut the frame components yourself or order them pre-cut from a lumberyard or home center, here's what you'll need to build the bench, backboard, umbrella rack, and cubby cabinet out of $1\frac{1}{8}$-in. (usually referred to as 1-in. nominal dimension) and $\frac{5}{8}$-in. veneered plywood, furniture grade:

Lumber List

Qty.	Desc.	Dimensions
1	Lid	$1\frac{1}{8}$ in. × 36 in. × 17 in.
1	Box bottom	$1\frac{1}{8}$ in. × 34 in. × 14 in.
1	Boot shelf	$1\frac{1}{8}$ in. × 36 in. × 16 in.
2	Sides	$1\frac{1}{8}$ in. × 16 in. × 16 in.
2	Box-frame panels	$1\frac{1}{8}$ in. × 34 in. × $5\frac{1}{2}$ in.
4	Brackets	$1\frac{1}{8}$ in. × 4-in. × 4-in. × 4-in. triangles
2	Umbrella racks	$1\frac{1}{8}$ in. × 16 in. × 6 in.
1	Backboard	$\frac{5}{8}$ in. × 48 in. × 32 in.
2	Cubby top/bottom	$\frac{5}{8}$ in. × 48 in. × 9 in.
2	Cubby sides	$\frac{5}{8}$ in. × 12 in. × 9 in.
3	Cubby dividers	$\frac{5}{8}$ in. × $12\frac{5}{8}$ in. × 9 in.

Labels on diagram:
Cubby top, Cubby side, Cubby divider, Cubby bottom, Backboard, Umbrella rack, Bracket, Lid, Side, Box frame panel, Box bottom, Boot shelf

▶ **DO** IT RIGHT

Remember the old adage, "measure twice, cut once"? Follow it to avoid making miscuts on your poplar panels. It may take little longer and seem tedious…until you mismeasure and cut a piece 1/8 in. too short. Keep this rule of thumb in mind, and you'll keep waste—and frustration—to a minimum.

▶ **LINGO**

Countersinking a screw or other fastener means to bury its head slightly below the surface so that it can be concealed with putty or a wooden plug. Get a countersink bit for your drill to countersink with ease.

Build the Boot Bench

1 **CUT THE PIECES.** Once you've found an adequate area for the bench and cubby assemblies (36 in. wide by 48 in. tall), set up a workstand or sawhorses and use the circular and miter saws to cut your frame components. Follow the Lumber List on p. 45.

2 **MAKE ROUTER GROOVES.** Rout two 1⅛-in.-wide by 3⅛-in.-deep grooves at 2 in. and 5½ in. from the bottom of the inside faces of each side panel of the boot bench. This will securely hold and support the edges of the boot shelf and the box bottom.

3 **FIT AND FASTEN.** Clamp one side of the boot bench to your workstand, drill three pilot holes in each side panel equidistant along the lengths of the grooves, and apply a bead of glue in one groove. Insert the panel for that groove (boot shelf or box bottom), and tap it in place with a rubber mallet; repeat with the other groove and panel. Glue the remaining side panel to the other ends of the shelf and bottom panels. Countersink 1½-in.-long flathead screws into the shelves to reinforce the glued joints and fasten the assembly. Square the assembly and, with a brad nailer, fasten the box-frame panels flush to the inside edges and tops of the side panels and to the bottom edge of the top shelf. Flip the assembly over and screw-fasten the other end of the frame components.

4 **ATTACH THE LID.** Screw-fasten the piano hinge to the edge of the lid through its precut holes, center the lid on the box, and screw-fasten the hinge to the inside face of the back box-frame panel. Attach a weight-rated hinge to each side of the piano hinge with the supplied countersunk screws, fill the screwhead holes with putty, let the putty dry overnight, then sand the filler smooth.

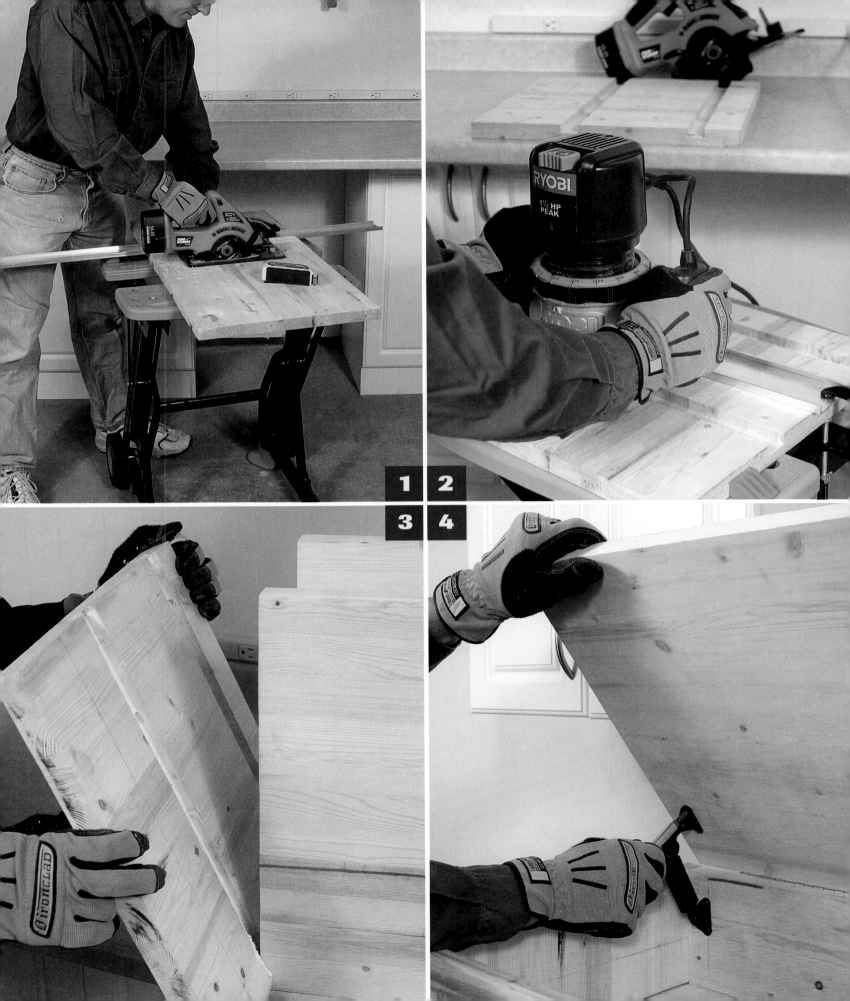

▶ DO IT RIGHT

Make sure you drill pilot holes vertically aligned to the center of the adjoining panel so that the wood screws have a good hold. Bend down so that your eye is level to the drill bit and check from right angles and from above to make sure the bit is headed straight before pulling the drill's trigger.

◑ NEED A HAND?

Positioning the cubby cabinet backboard against the wall is a three-person job; while two people hold the sides, the third person marks the stud locations, checks level, drills the pilot holes, and secures the lag bolts. Play it safe and make it a group effort.

Building a Cubby Cabinet

5 **ROUTER THE PANELS.** Measure $12\frac{5}{32}$ in., 24 in., and $35\frac{27}{32}$ in. down the length from one end of the cubby top and bottom panels, marking three points on each panel. Rout $\frac{5}{8}$-in.-wide by $\frac{5}{16}$-in.-deep grooves at the center of each mark for the cubby's dividers. Drill three pilot holes through the top panel, equidistant along each grooves' length.

6 **ASSEMBLE THE BOX.** Clamp one side panel to your workbench. Apply a bead of glue along the 9-in. edge of the top panel—grooves facing away from you—and position the panel against the corresponding side panel so that its edge rests flat on the workbench surface. Countersink $1\frac{1}{2}$-in.-long flathead wood screws in each of the predrilled pilot holes to join the two panels. Repeat with the bottom panel. When the top, bottom, and one side panel have been fastened, remove the assembly from the workbench, clamp the other side panel to the workbench, and fasten it in place to form the cubby box assembly.

7 **ADD THE DIVIDERS.** Use a rubber mallet to gently tap the three dividers into the box at the grooves until their edges are flush with the front edges of the box. With a brad nailer, nail three fasteners equidistant down each divider's length to fasten the dividers, securing the top panel, then the bottom. Square the assembly and attach the backboard.

8 **FINISH THE JOB.** Place a drop cloth under the boot bench and mask off the edges of the backboard. Fill and sand all fastener holes, sand the wood's surface smooth, and apply stain or primer to all of the cubby's and bench's exposed surfaces—remember to include the inside of the boot bench box. Add two coats of paint or at least two coats of stain over primer or sealer. For stained wood, apply two or more coats of polyurethane sealer after you apply the stain, and allow it to dry thoroughly before using the bench, cubbies, or hooks.

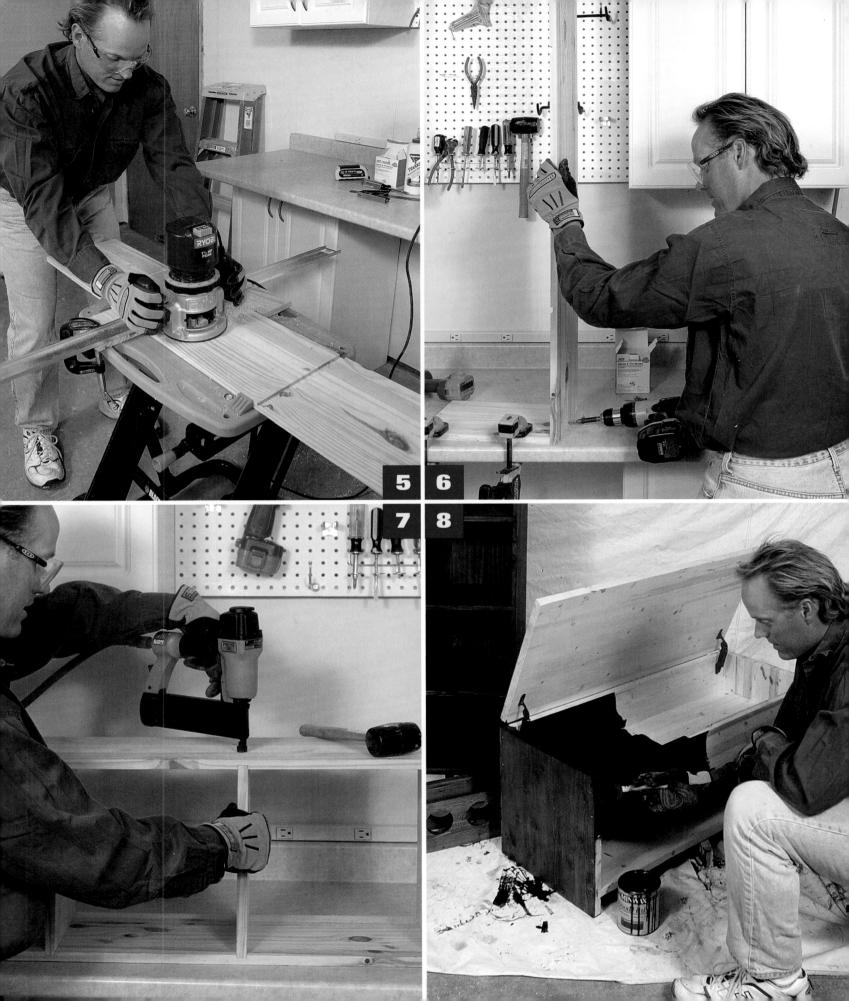

5 6

7 8

◆ DO IT NOW

Sand the holes of your two umbrella racks before you attach them to their brackets so you aren't fighting awkward angles later. Use a palm sander or your hand to work the sandpaper in and around the holes until they are completely smooth to the touch. With the sanding finished, nail the two umbrella racks to their brackets.

⁑ DO IT FAST

It's okay to make a slight mess when you're filling fastener holes with putty or wood paste. Work quickly, making sure to scrape away excess but not obsessing about neatness; once it dries, the filler sands off easily, even by hand.

Accessorize and Finish

9 **ADD THE SIDE BRACKETS.** Measure and mark 3 in. from each end on the inside face of the boot-bench box's sides. At the center of each pencil mark, hold the bracket 1⅛ in. below the top of the side (not the lid) and drill two pilot holes 1 in. apart through the side into each bracket. Use 1½-in. flat-head wood screws to secure the brackets to the sides of the boot bench.

10 **FASTEN THE UMBRELLA RACK.** Using your 3-in. hole-saw bit, cut three holes equidistant along the center of both umbrella rack panels, and sand them smooth. Center the umbrella rack panels over the brackets and flush to the top of the box, then use your brad nailer to secure the panels to the brackets. Fill the brad holes with putty, let the putty dry overnight, and sand it smooth.

11 **ADD THE HOOKS.** With a pencil, mark equally spaced locations for your coat hooks along the backboard, 6 in. below the bottom of the cubby cabinet. Use your level to mark a straight line, then drill pilot holes for the hooks. Attach the hooks using the fasteners provided.

12 **FASTEN THE BACKBOARD.** Position the backboard flush onto the top and sides of the back of the cubby cabinet. Use the brad nailer to fasten it every 6 in. along the perimeter. Lift the assembly into place on the wall so that the bottom of the cubby cabinet will be centered 36 in. over the top of the boot bench when it is in place. Use your tape measure and pencil to mark the wall stud locations; check that the cubby cabinet is level, and drill two pilot holes through the backboard, 8 in. from the top and bottom edges, for lag screws to pass into each stud. Countersink the pilot holes up to 1/16 in. deep. Make a final check for level, and screw the backboard to the wall with a socket wrench. Fill all fastener holes with wood paste or putty, let dry overnight, then sand smooth.

9 10

11 12

You know better than anyone else what your family needs in a multipurpose storage solution, so personalize this project with a few creative and inexpensive alterations. If you want an out-of-sight spot to hide your dirty shoes and boots, then build a deep chest instead of displaying them on an open shelf below the bench. Or swap out a few coat hooks for some pegs that you can hang your hat on. If you think the cubbies will become a black hole for who-knows-what, a simple shelf will suffice. While it's important to follow the fastening rules, the style is up to you.

There are a variety of alternative storage ideas to incorporate in this project: add baskets in the cubbies, place an upholstered cushion on the seat, build a simple shelf instead of a cabinet, or use more hooks or pegs for coat hangers.

A bin rack is another option to consider when upgrading an entry. Choose a rack that has a high lip on the bins to help keep loose items from falling out of the bins.

If you don't have space for a deep organizer unit, at least hang up a coat rack. One that is also a picture-frame hanger will guide young children's hands to their own coat hooks.

Many different styles of coat hooks are available from a variety of sources. Choose brass or wrought iron, chrome or pewter; hooks with artistic designs are available as well.

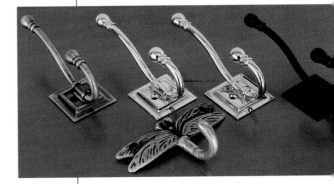

If space permits beneath the bench, use baskets to conceal mittens, boots or garden clogs. The loosely woven wicker sides of the baskets permit warm air to pass through, drying any damp objects inside them.

Workshop Solution

Transform a bare garage wall into a multipurpose **WORKSHOP AREA** featuring cabinets, work surface, & electrical outlets

FOR MANY FOLKS, A GARAGE OFTEN DOUBLES AS A WORK AREA for hobbies and light-duty home improvement projects. This multipurpose workshop area will create a space where everything is organized and within easy reach—and it's easy to build on a base of ready-to-assemble cabinets. The cabinets are lockable, so they can keep sharp tools, paints, and solvents child-safe. Add a generous work surface and a handy pegboard to the setup and you'll enjoy even more utility and convenience. All it takes is a little carpentry skill and a spare Saturday to transform a blank wall or corner into a useful workshop.

| ASSEMBLE THE CABINETS | HANG THE CABINETS | SET THE COUNTERTOP | ADD ELECTRICAL OUTLET |

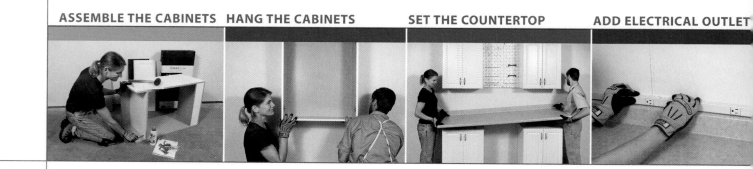

▷ LINGO

MDF is an acronym for medium-density fiberboard, a composite wood made from wood fibers glued under heat and pressure that is denser and stiffer than solid woods such as oak and pine. RTA is shorthand used by cabinet parts manufacturers; it means ready to assemble.

◆ DO IT NOW

Before you purchase cabinets, make sure you've got the space and the clearances to accommodate them. Be sure vehicles will still fit in the garage once the workshop is finished, and that the doors of the upper cabinets can swing under or are clear of the garage door and its track or springs.

Tools & Gear

The ready-to-assemble (RTA) cabinets are built quickly and installed easily with a basic set of tools, including these items:

DRILL. You'll need one of these to drive in the lag screws that secure the cabinets to the wall. In addition to a set of drill and screwdriver bits, consider a socket set (see COOL TOOL, below).

CARPENTRY TOOLS. Keep on hand a 12-oz. hammer, rubber mallet, hand saw, combination square, measuring tape, carpenter's pencil, and 4-ft.-long carpenter's level.

STUD FINDER. This electronic tool makes it easy to find the wall studs behind wallboard for attaching the cabinets.

ELECTRICAL TOOLS. Use a voltage tester, both lineman's and needle-nose pliers, electrical tape, and wire nuts to extend a circuit in the garage to the workshop area.

STEPLADDER. You'll need this to safely hold the upper cabinets in place as you attach them to the wall.

COOL TOOL

A **set of sockets** for your drill makes it easier and faster to drive lag screws and other hexagonal-headed fasteners than you could with a manual socket wrench. Each socket features a stem similar to a drill or screw bit that fits and tightens in the drill's chuck. Sockets are sold in metric or standard fractional measurements (e.g., $3/4$ in.), so choose a set the same size as the dimensions of the lag screws that come in the cabinet package you purchase.

What to Buy

1| READY-TO-ASSEMBLE (RTA) CABINETS. For lasting durability, look for solid wood or medium-density fiberboard (MDF) construction—as opposed to pressed wood or particleboard—on the box panels, frames, doors, and drawers.

2| FASTENERS. Unless supplied with the cabinets, get a small box of 2-in. lag screws to attach them to the wall. For the 1×2 frame, use 3-in. lag screws to fasten the frame to the studs. Use wood glue and ¾-in. wood screws to attach the pegboard to its frame.

3| PEGBOARD AND HOOKS. You'll need a 24-in. by 48-in. piece of pegboard and a set of hooks to hang your small tools.

4| 1×2 LUMBER AND SHIMS. You'll use a pair of 8-ft. lengths to frame the pegboard and a bundle of wood or composite shims to level the base cabinets, if necessary.

5| COUNTERTOP. Go with a premade laminate countertop over a composite wood substrate, sold in standard dimensions and easily attached to RTA cabinets.

6| WIRE MOLD AND OUTLET STRIP. You may need a wire mold—a flexible, prewired plastic channel—to extend wires from the nearest junction box to a 6-ft.-long strip of electrical outlets mounted across the back of the countertop.

A READY-IN-MINUTES WORKSHOP

Pairs of premade wall and base cabinets, a laminate countertop, and a pegboard panel combine to make a tidy workbench with convenient tool and material storage that fits neatly against a garage sidewall. Kits that contain complete RTA cabinets you can assemble in minutes means that your workshop will be finished and ready for your use in record time. Always check the parts list; inventory the components, fasteners, and supplied tools; and follow the manufacturer's directions for the best result when you assemble factory cabinets.

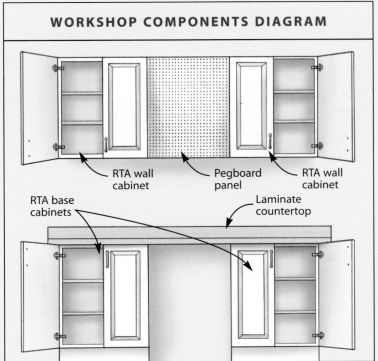

WORKSHOP COMPONENTS DIAGRAM

RTA wall cabinet

Pegboard panel

RTA wall cabinet

RTA base cabinets

Laminate countertop

➕ **WHAT CAN GO WRONG**

If your garage walls have a concrete foundation curb, you'll have to cut out the back and sides of the cabinet box to fit over it. This extra step requires some precision and perhaps refinishing. If possible, choose a wall for your workshop without a curb.

◆ **DO IT NOW**

If you plan to refinish your garage floor with epoxy paint (see Durable Floor Finish, pp. 110–117), finish that project before you add a workshop. If you wait until the workshop is in place, you'll have to refinish around the base cabinets, which might mar their surfaces or make for a less-than-ideal floor finish. Use sheets of cardboard or butcher paper to protect the new floor finish as you assemble this workshop.

Assemble the Cabinets

1 **LOCATE AN AREA.** Look for a blank wall with one or two existing electrical outlets and, if possible, no foundation curb (see WHAT CAN GO WRONG, left). The space should be 78 in. across, 30 in. deep, and 72 in. tall. Use a stud finder to locate each wall-frame member behind the wallboard; with a 4-ft. carpenter's level and a pencil, mark along the length of each stud within the project area.

2 **BUILD THE CABINET BOXES.** Working one cabinet at a time, remove all the components of the RTA cabinet from their shipping box and check them against the list provided with the assembly instructions, along with any hardware, fasteners, and tools. Read and follow the manufacturer's instructions exactly to assemble the four cabinets, repeating this process with each unit.

3 **READY THE DOORS.** Add door hinges and drawer hardware, as directed by the manufacturer. Attach the hardware first to the door, then to the cabinet's walls. Mount and test the operation of the doors and drawers, and adjust them, if necessary, so they swing or slide open, close smoothly, and are flush to the cabinet frames with their latches secure.

4 **PROTECT THE FINISHES.** Once you are satisfied with the doors' and drawers' operation, remove them, as well as any adjustable shelving inside the cabinets, and set them aside in a safe place, where they will be protected from damage as you move and install the units on the wall. This makes the cabinet boxes lighter and easier to transport and shim, ensuring a good result. Most concealed hingesets have release clips that facilitate easy removal and reattachment of the doors without unscrewing the hinges from the cabinets or doors.

1

2

3

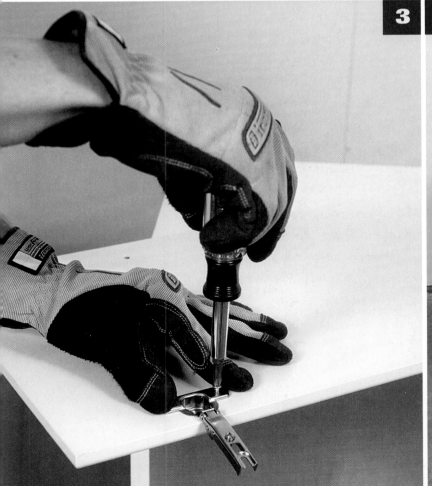

4

◑ NEED A HAND?

Even without its doors or drawers, a storage cabinet can become heavy or awkward to hold in place as you level and plumb it, back it up to a wall stud, and set it squarely over a base cabinet—much less fasten it. Have a helper hold it in place, and adjust it as you position and install it, saving time and preventing mistakes.

＋ WHAT CAN GO WRONG

If the back of a cabinet covers an existing electrical outlet, use your measuring tape and pencil to transfer its location to the inside back panel of the cabinet. Then cut out a hole to fit the outlet box, using a drill bit on your drill to make starter holes at two of the marked corners, followed by a small hand or power jig saw to cut the hole's straight lines.

Build the Workshop

5 **HANG THE BASE CABINETS.** Place the base cabinets 24 in. apart, with at least one wall stud running behind each cabinet. Adjust the first cabinet for level, checking with a carpenter's level and adding shims under the frame, if necessary. Drill three pilot holes through the back of the cabinet box and wallboard into the stud, then drive in 2-in. lag screws or the supplied fasteners to secure the cabinet to the wall. Do not over-tighten the fasteners. Measure 24 in. across, position the other base cabinet, then install it the same way; use your level across both cabinets as you shim to ensure a level surface for the countertop (see Step 9, p. 62).

6 **HANG THE WALL CABINETS.** With a helper, lift and place a wall cabinet directly over a base cabinet. Use your carpenter's level to check that it is plumb—vertically straight—and level. Make pencil marks at the top, bottom, and sides of the cabinet for reference. Measure from the nearest corner to the stud and use your pencil to transfer the stud's location to the inside back panel of the cabinet.

Drill three pilot holes through the back of the cabinet box and wallboard into the stud, then drive in 2-in. lag screws or the supplied fasteners to attach the cabinet to the wall; avoid overtightening the fasteners. Repeat for the second cabinet, checking for level and spacing to the other cabinets.

7 **FRAME AND INSTALL THE PEGBOARD.** Measure the area between the two wall cabinets; it should be 24 in. wide by 30 in. tall. Cut the pegboard on a table saw or with a circular saw to fit the space. Measure and cut 1×2 lumber to frame the perimeter of the pegboard's back. Attach the frame flush with the pegboard's outside edges, using wood glue and wood screws every 6 in. around its perimeter. Position the assembly on the wall and drive lag screws through the pegboard, its frame, and the wallboard into the wall studs.

8 **FINISH WITH HOOKS.** Attach removable hooks, shelves, fittings, and other small tool hangers to the pegboard.

5

6

7

8

▶ **LINGO**

A backsplash is a 3-in.- to 4-in.-high vertical piece along the back edge of many premade countertops. It helps contain any spills, debris, tools, or fasteners from falling behind the countertop.

◆ **DO** IT NOW

Check the available amperage of the circuit you intend to extend before connecting a new outlet strip at an outlet or junction box. You'll find the amperage of the circuit on the circuit breaker or fuse in the main service panel. If there's not enough amps to power a full strip, consider a shorter strip or simply mount one or two new outlets on the wall above the countertop and extend service to them.

Finish the Job

9 **ATTACH THE COUNTERTOP.** The base cabinets either allow for fastening the countertop through the cabinets' tops or feature preinstalled cleats at each corner for this purpose. Position and shim the laminate countertop over the base cabinets and against the wall, then loosely fasten it

to the cabinets from the underside with lag screws. Set each screw once all of them have been started, tightening them flush with the wood's surface.

10 **FIND THE SOURCE.** Locate the nearest electrical outlet or junction box and turn off power to its circuit at the service panel, then remove its cover and expose the wires. Follow the steps for extending electrical service on pp. 16–17. Mount clamps for the outlet strip. It's best either to fit the outlet strip flush to one end or to center it, then fasten it to the wall with screws at each stud location; you should have stud locations marked every 16 in. or 24 in. along the strip's 6-ft. length.

11 **ATTACH THE OUTLET STRIP.** Fit the outlet strip along the back edge of the countertop or backsplash. If the garage walls are covered with wallboard or made of concrete blocks, install a wire mold as a bridge from the nearest outlet or junction box to the outlet strip; it will protect and hide the wires.

12 **CONNECT THE CIRCUIT.** Connect the outlet strip's wires, following the instructions in the outlet strip's package (see Step 3, p. 16). Turn on the circuit and test the outlet with a voltage tester before pushing the wires back into the junction box and attaching its cover. Finally, reattach the cabinet doors, drawers, and shelving to complete the project, making sure they still swing or slide open, close smoothly, and rest flush and flat with the cabinet boxes. Adjust the shelves inside the cabinets as necessary to accommodate your storage needs. Mount and plug in accessory lighting.

9 10
11 12

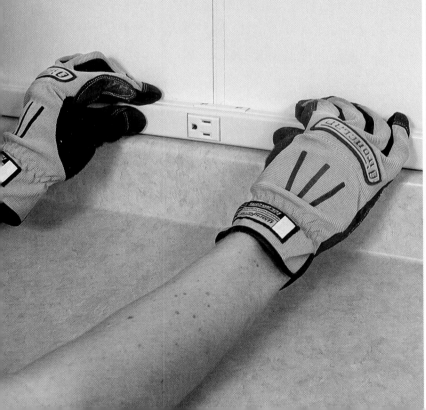

Your own garage workshop has never been easier. A quick web search or trip to your nearest home improvement store will reveal a variety of RTA cabinets and countertops in a range of sizes to suit any taste, special need, or available space. You also have a choice of small tool hangers if a pegboard isn't your style, including magnetic strips and slotted racks that fit a number of tools and gear, and which fasten easily and quickly to the wall. Don't forget to incorporate other benchtop organizers, such as bins, baskets, shelves, and book and magazine holders.

Specialty hanging racks (above) are the right choice to give easy access to frequently needed tools. Another choice worth considering is a magnetic bar rack (below) that holds steel and iron tools.

Use a ready-made leg assembly to support one end of a countertop and a cabinet for the other. An adjustable stool on rollers makes working at close range a snap.

This complete auto shop setup has drawer cabinets to hold an assortment of large and small shop tools, a large work surface, a pegboard rack for hand tools, and wall storage for large equipment, such as an under-car creeper and an airtight receptacle for the safe disposal of oily rags.

Organize your wrenches, pliers, screwdrivers, saws, and hammers by size to make finding them easy. Outline each tool with a marking pen to make it easy to spot its place on the pegboard.

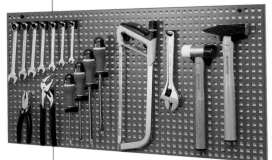

Use a cabinet with both large bins and smaller cubbyholes to hold tools, materials, and partially finished projects. Look for a unit with deep bins and a raised lip, or choose one that has slanted openings to hold objects inside.

Heavy-gauge legs and strong braces mean an unshakeable workbench. Choose one that bolts together if storing the bench flat between uses is a necessity.

Trash Barrel Shed

Conceal a pair of trash or recycling containers with an easy-to-build **LEAN-TO SHED** that looks great on the side of the garage

A DMIT IT: YOU CAN'T STAND THE SIGHT OF YOUR TRASH CANS, especially as you drive up your driveway and see them alongside the garage. A necessary evil, right? No more. Now you can conceal them in an attractive, inexpensive, and easy-to-build shed that requires basic skills, tools, and materials. In a weekend, your trash cans will have a home of their own that keeps them within easy reach for their weekly trip to the curb. Open the top of the shed to fill the cans, and remove them through the front doors. The low-profile design is sized for a pair of 30-gal. molded plastic trash cans, while the exterior finishes blend with the house, making the bins all but disappear from view.

CUT THE PIECES

CONSTRUCT THE FRAME

BUILD THE DOORS

FINISH THE SHED

Consider renting a pneumatic (or compressed air-driven) nail gun. It requires some practice to get a feel for it but provides for fast, easy, and precise fastening, especially with angled and narrow pieces. It's the experienced carpenter's choice.

Tools & Gear

In addition to your basic tool set (see pp. 6–7), buy or rent the following gear:

CIRCULAR SAW. A lightweight cordless version with a plywood-cutting blade is easier and safer to handle in tight spaces than a corded version.

TABLE SAW. Rent or borrow one to make straight and beveled cuts on the siding and roof panels (see Lumber List, right).

COMPOUND MITER SAW. Rent this tool for making precise angled cuts on your lumber (see COOL TOOL, below).

T-BEVEL OR PROTRACTOR. Use one or the other for measuring and transferring angles to your cut stock.

COMBINATION SQUARE. This adjustable tool allows you to draw straight lines on 2×4s to help guide your cuts. Also use it to check that adjacent framing members are square to each other. It usually features a handy 12-in. ruler and a straightedge for small measuring and marking tasks.

CAULKING GUN. You'll need one to apply tubes of adhesive to the siding panels.

When building outdoor projects, use pressure-treated (PT) lumber instead of standard, untreated lumber. PT lumber contains low-toxicity chemicals that protect the wood from rot and insects, especially where it contacts the ground or damp concrete. It's a little heavier and denser than standard lumber, but lasts longer than untreated wood.

COOL TOOL

A **compound miter saw** is a circular saw mounted on a steel base for cutting lumber that is less than 5 in. wide. Like all power saws, this tool requires your full attention and respect. Set your 2-by lumber against the base's back rail, line up your pencil mark with the projected laser cut line, squeeze the trigger to start the blade, and then slowly draw it down to make the most precise straight, angle, and/or bevel cut possible.

What to Buy

1| 2×4 PRESSURE-TREATED LUMBER. The non-toxic treatment outweighs the slight price premium. You'll need eight 8-ft. pieces to satisfy the Lumber List (below).

2| T-111 SIDING. Sold in 4-ft. by 8-ft. panels; try to match or complement your home's existing exterior finishes. You'll need three panels for the project.

3| SHEATHING PANELS. Buy one 4-ft. by 8-ft. sheet of ⁵⁄₈-in. exterior-grade plywood for the roof lid and doors.

4| FASTENERS AND ADHESIVE. You'll need small boxes of 10d common nails, 2-in. wood or deck screws, and roofing nails plus a dozen 2-in. lag screws. You'll need a tube or two of waterproof construction adhesive, as well.

5| PRIMER AND PAINT. Use an exterior-grade latex primer and paint that matches or complements the color of your home's exterior finish. A quart of primer and a gallon of paint should be more than enough for two coats.

6| ROOFING. Use materials compatible with your home's roof materials; you'll need enough for a 4-ft. by 3-ft. surface. Get a metal drip edge, too.

7| HARDWARE. You'll need six 3½-in. T-hinges, a pair of door pulls, and a latch or hasp for the doors. Buy four dozen ¾-in. flat-head bolts, nuts, and washers and a dozen flat-head, 2-in. machine screws that are matched to the diameter of the hinges' holes. Make sure all the hardware is galvanized.

TRASH BARREL SHED DIAGRAM

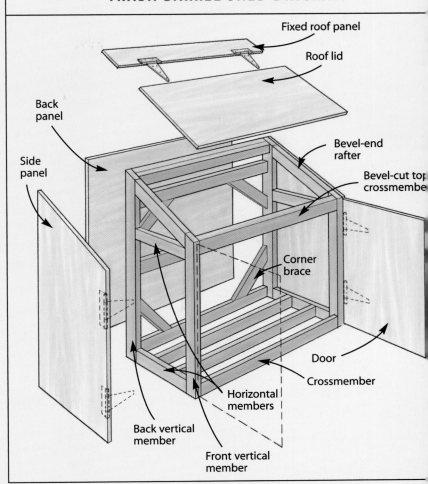

Fixed roof panel

Roof lid

Back panel

Bevel-end rafter

Bevel-cut top crossmember

Side panel

Corner brace

Door

Crossmember

Horizontal members

Back vertical member

Front vertical member

Lumber list

Qty.	Desc.	Dimensions
2	Back vertical members	2 in. × 4 in. × 54 in. (at their highest point; mark and cut 30° angles at the top—see Step 1, p. 70).
2	Front vertical members	2 in. × 4 in. × 42 in. (cut 30° angles at top)
4	Horizontal members	2 in. × 4 in. × 17 in.
2	Rafters	2 in. × 4 in. × 27 in. (mark and cut each end at parallel 40° angles—see Step 1, p. 70).
3	Top crossmembers	2 in. × 4 in. × 43¾ in. (bevel top edge 30°)
6	Crossmembers	2 in. × 4 in. × 43¾ in.
4	Corner braces	2 in. × 4 in. × 18 in. (cut 45° angles on each end)
2	Side panels	24 in. × 60 in. T-111 plywood (cut to fit)
1	Back panel	48 in. × 54 in. T-111 plywood (cut to fit exact dimensions before fastening to the frame members)
1	Fixed roof panel	48 in. × 6 in. plywood
1	Roof lid	48 in. × 21 in. plywood
1	Door stock	41⅞ in. × 48 in. T-111 plywood

❶ NEED A HAND?

This project will be easier to build if you use a flat and stable elevated work table made from a 4-ft. by 8-ft. sheet of ⅝-in. plywood attached with screws to two or three supporting sawhorses. Not only will getting materials off the ground save your knees and back, but it will also provide some clearance as you cut and fasten the framing members. Disassemble and store the work table when the project is complete.

▪ LINGO

The term "at grade" refers to the surface or level of the ground, specifically, the existing or proposed level or elevation you'll use as a starting point from which to measure or build up. Something "at grade" is considered to be at ground level.

Build the Frame

1 **CUT THE FRAME MEMBERS.** On a flat surface (see NEED A HAND?, left), cut all of the framing members with a circular or compound miter saw. To determine angle cuts on the vertical members and rafters, lay out one side assembly, lay a rafter under it, and mark the vertical members and the rafter for the angle cuts. Use the miter saw to cut the angles, then use the cut rafter as a template to mark and cut the second rafter and the other tall vertical member of the other side assembly to the same angles.

2 **BUILD THE SIDE ASSEMBLIES.** Drill pilot holes and use wood screws to fasten the horizontal and vertical members for both sides together. Screw the rafters to the vertical members to complete the side frames. If the shed's site is unpaved, make a 2-ft. by 4-ft. pad using 8-in. by 12-in. by 16-in. concrete pavers set on flat, compacted dirt or pea gravel to serve as a stable, at-grade platform. Move the side assemblies to the site.

3 **JOIN THE ASSEMBLIES.** If you rented a power nailer, it can be used to fasten the assemblies, or you can drill pilot holes and use wood screws. Fasten the side frames to the crossmembers (see Lumber List and Trash Barrel Shed Diagram, p. 69). Finally, install and fasten the corner braces, completing the shed frame assembly.

4 **CUT THE SIDING PANELS.** Cut the T-111 siding to create two, 2-ft. by 5-ft. sides. Stand these cut panels against the side frames and mark the rafter angle along the top (narrow) edge on the panels' back faces. Use a table or circular saw to cut each side panel along the marked angle. Measure and cut the shed's back panel from the other sheet of T-111 siding with a table or circular saw.

1

2

3

4

➕ WHAT CAN GO WRONG

Construction adhesive dries fast, so only apply it to the frame members one side at a time, and be ready to attach the siding panels to the frame within two to three minutes of applying the glue. If the glue forms a skin, it will be unable to bond to the panel.

▶ DO IT RIGHT

You'll want to be precise when you cut the doors, so use a straightedge held to the table with clamps to guide the saw as you make the cut on your pencil mark. Take it slow and steady until the blade is completely clear of the panel's end.

Attach the Sides and Doors

5 **APPLY THE SIDING.** Apply construction adhesive to the outside faces of one side frame assembly; position and screw a side panel in place using deck screws spaced every 8 in. Repeat the process with the other side panel. Apply adhesive to the outside back crossmembers, then position and screw the back panel to the frame.

6 **CUT THE DOOR STOCK.** You'll need to leave a ⅛-in. gap between the doors, so here's a trick: cut the door panel (see Lumber List p. 69) exactly in half using a saw guide (see DO IT RIGHT, left); the ⅛-in. kerf (or width) of the saw blade will remove enough wood to provide the necessary gap between two equal-size doors.

7 **HANG THE DOORS.** On a flat work surface, set a T-hinge 8 in. from the top and bottom of each door, and use your pencil to mark the location of the bolt holes on the doors' outer surface. Drill holes at the marks and secure the hinges to the door using flat-head bolts fastened with washers and nuts on the backsides of the doors. With a helper holding a door in place on the shed, align the door flush to the top of the side frame, then check that it is level, with a ⅛-in. clearance at the bottom. Use your pencil to mark the screw-hole locations for the other hinge flanges on the side frames, then drill pilot holes and attach the hinges with flat-head galvanized machine screws. Repeat with the other door, and check the doors' operation; they should swing out freely.

8 **ADD THE HARDWARE.** Position a door pull 2 in. from the opening and 5 in. from the top of each door, so that the two pulls are level with each other; position the latching post-safety hasp across the opening. Use the screws provided with the door hardware to attach the hasp and pulls. This type of latch keeps the front doors closed and secure, but easily accessible—you'll need to operate the hasp when you open the shed doors to remove the cans on pickup day.

5 6

7 8

Its always best to prime or seal unfinished wood before applying a finish coat of paint, especially for a shed that will be exposed to the weather. If your time is limited or you don't have primer paint handy, just apply two coats of the finish paint or use leftover exterior-grade paint from a previous project instead of the primer.

:: DO IT FAST

+ WHAT CAN GO WRONG

Without a metal drip edge, water running off the sloped roof will wick back up the wood panel lid, causing it to swell and possibly delaminate, form mold, and become unsightly or decay. The drip edge ensures that run-off will fall harmlessly to the ground.

Fit the Hinged Roof

9 **FASTEN THE FIXED ROOF PANEL.** Cut and fasten the fixed roof panel to the top of the frame and rafters using wood screws every 8 in. across the length of the panel and 1 in. from its corners.

10 **FIT THE ROOF LID.** Measure and cut the roof lid so it fits flush to the finished sides of the shed frame, tight against the fixed panel (see Step 11, below), with a 1-in. overhang along the front of the frame.

11 **ATTACH THE HINGES.** Position two T-hinges across the fixed roof panel and the roof lid, 12 in. from each side of the shed. Use your pencil to mark the location of the bolt holes, then drill pilot holes and fasten the hinges with washers and nuts concealed  on the underside of the lid. Check the lid's operation—you should be able to easily lift it up with one hand and allow it to remain in the "up" position as you put trash into the containers within the shed.

12 **ROOF AND PAINT.** Using a material that matches or is complementary to your home's existing roof, attach the roofing material to the lid and fixed panel, covering the hinges but leaving a ⅜-in. gap where the panels join for clearance when the lid is opened and closed (a little rain may penetrate the joint, but most garbage and recycling containers are weatherproof, and the shed will shelter them from most rainfall). If you use asphalt shingles, lap the courses to hide most nail heads; cover any exposed nail heads with plastic asphalt cement. Prime and paint the doors and siding of the shed to match or complement your home; apply two to three coats to each to achieve the proper coverage and color. As an option, you can prime and paint the shed's wooden roof instead of applying shingles or another roofing finish.

9 10

11 12

Composition shingles (below) are a good choice for a weather-resistant roof on your trash barrel shed. They come in many colors and textures. Pick a paint or stain color (right) that matches your garage's exterior.

The first consideration for any outdoor building project adjacent to your home is to choose a design that complements the main structure's scale, design, and finish materials. For a waste station alongside your garage, make it look like it belongs on and with the house so it doesn't scream for attention. Once you choose a style and materials, make the shed as practical as you want; consider a handy shelf for extra trash and yard bags; decorative trim on the shed's sides, doors, or roof; or door mechanisms that make the door easier to open than this project's out-swing door design allows.

Make moving heavy trash cans an easy task on trash day by storing them on a wheeled cart that will carry them to the curb. Omit the lower crossmember behind the doors of the shed to park the trash barrel cart inside it.

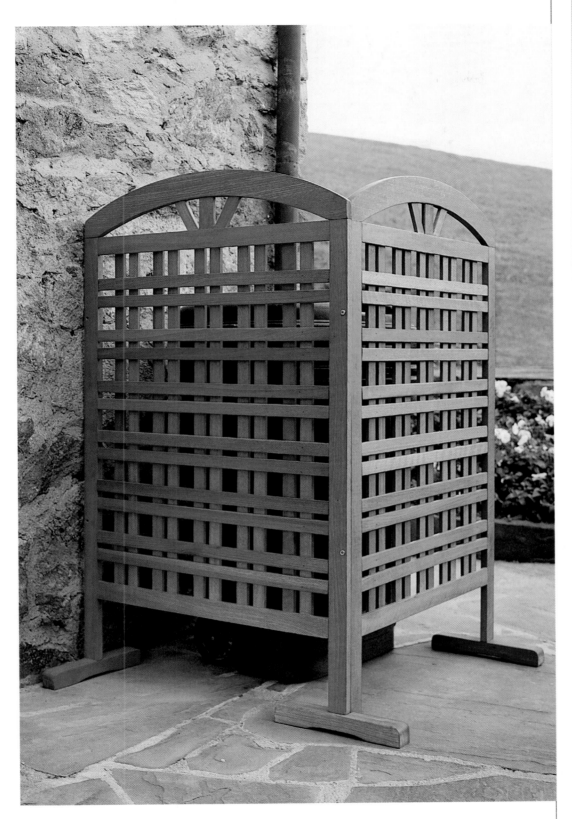

Make recycling plastic grocery bags a snap by hanging a bag sleeve on a cuphook inside the trash barrel shed's door. Stuff bags in the top and pull them out of the bottom when you need one.

Crush aluminum and steel cans to conserve space in your bins and reduce the number of trips to the recycling center.

Durable and decorative screens made of teak or cypress are another choice for concealing trash cans. Choose a model that has wide feet for stability. You'll need to refresh its surface with teak oil or a new coat of waterproof stain and sealant each year.

Wall-Mounted Storage System

Use these wall-mounted SLOTTED PANELS to create an attractive combination of storage solutions and work areas

YOU WANT THE "ULTIMATE" GARAGE but aren't sure you possess the skills (or the funds) to get it. It's actually well within your reach, thanks to an easy-to install wall-mounted panel system. The slotted panels allow you to hang a variety of cabinets, bins, shelves, hooks, and other storage fixtures and accessories, and they install with basic tools and common fasteners. In fact, most slotted panel systems (also called slatwall systems) have an interlocking design, which not only installs fast and straight, but also delivers additional stability by locking together. Plus, these systems are adaptable, enabling you to add or replace storage components to meet your changing needs.

LAY OUT THE SYSTEM	MAKE THE CUT OUTS	ATTACH THE PANELS	ADD THE ACCESSORIES

❖ **COOL TOOL**

A chalk line draws a long, straight line across any surface with one quick snap. The colored chalk dust inside the tool's metal or plastic box sticks to the string as you pull it out. Use a nail to hold one end on your pencil mark while you draw out the string line, align it with your other mark, lift up the string in the middle, and snap it to mark your chalk line.

▶ **DO** IT RIGHT

This panel system is fastened to the wall with standard deck or wallboard screws, but they must "bite" at least 1 in. into the wall studs for a secure hold. For an open stud wall, use 1½-in.-long screws; for walls covered by ½-in. or ⅝-in. wallboard, use 2-in. screws.

Tools & Gear

Everything you need to locate and install this system is in your basic tool box (see pp. 6–7), including the following:

DRILL. A corded tool or 18-volt cordless drill and a complete set of bits and hole-saw blades will drive the screws into the wall studs and bore holes for cutouts.

STUD FINDER. Consider a model with an AC finder to detect the location of electrical wires, as well as the wall studs.

POWER SAWS. You'll need a circular saw with a plywood-cutting blade and a jig saw for cutting holes mid-panel.

CLAMPS. Use an adjustable clamp to hold two panels together while you fasten the other end of an unattached panel.

CARPENTER'S LEVEL. Use a 4-ft. level to make sure the panels are straight.

CHALK LINE. This tool gives you a long, straight line from which to locate the first panel.

FRAMING SQUARE. Use this tool to help ensure straight panel cuts.

UTILITY KNIFE. You'll need this tool (with a fresh blade) to cut and notch the trim pieces.

STEPLADDER. A must-have for a safe work environment.

COOL TOOL

Not all circular or table saw blades are created equal. In fact, there's quite a variation depending on what's being cut. For plywood and other panel materials—including these slotted panels—choose a hardened steel blade with at least 200 teeth in total to make a nice, clean cut free of surface mars or splinters. Keep the blade sharp to reduce its resistance as it cuts, which also extends the life of your saw's motor and cordless tool battery. Saw blades are available wherever saws are sold.

What to Buy

1| SLOTTED PANELS. The panels measure 12 in. by 96 in. each and are sold in packs of two panels, so you'll need eight packs for this project. Get the trim packages, too, to fit around any outlet cutouts and window or door openings.

2| SLOTTED CHANNEL TRACK. This 6-in.-wide by 48-in.-long single channel is designed for a pair of gear hooks.

3| SCREWS. Buy a large (100 ct.) box of #8 wallboard or coated deck screws; see DO IT RIGHT, left, to determine the length of the screws you'll need to hold the panels and track in place.

4| WALL-MOUNTED GEAR BOXES. We selected one 24-in.-tall single-door cabinet and one 30-in.-tall double-door storage case to hang along the wall in the panel grooves.

5| MOBILE GEAR BOXES. This project calls for two gear boxes (one with two doors, the other with five rows of drawers), plus two 5-ft.-tall, two-door tall storage cabinets, all on lockable casters for mobility.

6| ACCESSORIES. Purchase a 48-in.-wide shelf, a 6-ft.-long workbench (on lockable casters), 19-in. and 27-in. baskets, and a deep hook and a big hook to complete the system.

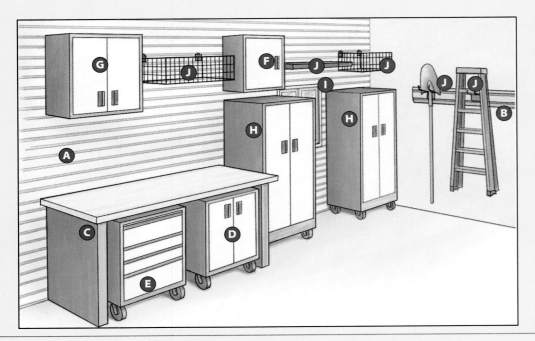

COMPONENT KEY

This diagram identifies the various system components:

A: GearWall™ (slotted) panels

B: GearTrack™ channel

C: 6-ft. modular workbench

D: Modular GearBox

E: Modular GearDrawers

F: 24-in. Wall GearBox

G: 30-in. Wall GearBox

H: Tall GearBox

I: GearWall trim

J: Accessories (baskets, hooks, and shelves)

▶ DO IT RIGHT

Don't guess when making cutouts for windows, doors, and electrical switches or outlets. Measure and mark their locations on the panels carefully, or use a roll of butcher or Kraft paper to create a template that you can transfer onto the panel before you cut into it.

◆ DO IT NOW

For installations over 20 ft., slotted panel manufacturers suggest cutting the panels mid-length—4 ft.—to stagger the vertical joints for better looks and greater stability. If you stagger joints by making cuts at other spots in the panels, make sure to cut the panels to the same lengths as your wall stud spacing to maintain maximum hold to the wall.

Lay Out and Cut the Panels

1 **FIND A PLACE.** This project requires an 8-ft. wall at least 21 ft. long (most garages are over 22 ft. long), with enough clearance in front of the GearBoxes to allow their doors and drawers to open freely into the garage. Assuming the walls are finished with  wallboard, use the stud/AC finder to locate and mark the wall studs and electrical wires (to avoid piercing wires passing through studs). Use the level and pencil to mark each stud along its length and along any wire runs.

2 **LAY OUT THE PANELS.** Starting from the front corner of the garage, lay out uncut full-sized panels as two vertical columns, eight panels deep, with a single vertical seam where the two columns meet. The joint will be concealed by the 24-in. wall-mounted GearBox and the tall modular GearBox (see pp. 86–87). The GearTrack channel will be installed on the end of the second row at the proper height for your tools.

3 **MARK FOR THE OPENINGS.** Use your tape measure and pencil to create a paper template (see DO IT RIGHT, left) or a scaled sketch showing the precise location and dimensions of any windows, doors, and electrical outlets or switches within the area to be paneled. Carefully transfer those locations to the panels that need to be cut, checking your pencil marks against the template or sketch a few times.

4 **CUT THE OPENINGS.** For each opening, use a fine-tooth, 1-in. hole saw blade to drill into  opposite corners of your marked cutout, then use the jig saw with a fine-tooth blade to carefully cut out the rest of the opening along the pencil mark. Tip: Round each corner, then come back to cut the sharp corner angles after you cut out the opening.

1   **2**
3   **4**

If your garage wall isn't exactly flush or straight, you might need a clamp to hold a new panel up to the one you just fastened to the wall. Use the slotted tracks in the panels to clamp the two panels together on one end while you fasten the other end to the wall studs with screws.

⋮ LINGO

The sharp point and deep threads of self-tapping screws enable them to pierce the surface of the materials into which they are being driven (such as a plastic panel) without the need for drilling a pilot hole.

Attach the Panels

5 **SNAP YOUR LINE.** At a convenient height on the wall, snap a level, 16-ft. chalk line from the front corner of the garage. Measure from the chalk line to the ceiling and use a pencil to mark the lowest point on the ceiling. From this low point, measure down 12¼ in. and snap a level, 16-ft. chalk line extending from the front corner of the garage to the other end of the project area.

6 **ALIGN THE FIRST PANEL.** Place the first panel with its tongue edge up and its bottom—or grooved—edge lined up with the upper chalk line and with one end abutting the front corner of the garage. Mark the length of the other end with a pencil for reference. Use your level to check along the bottom edge and make sure the panel is straight.

7 **FASTEN THE FIRST PANEL.** Starting at one top corner and working lengthwise, use self-tapping deck or wallboard screws along and within the panel's slotted groove to fasten the panel at each wall stud location, using the stud locations you marked in Step 1. Once you reach the end of the panel, drop to the next slotted grove and work lengthwise across the panel to the other end until the panel is completely attached.

8 **INSTALL THE REMAINING PANELS AND TRIM.** Once the first panel is installed, the rest are easy. Simply align the new panel's end and shove its upper tongue edge into the bottom groove of the panel above it. A helper can hold the loose panel in place as you fasten it, or use a clamp. With each course, check that the panels are level, and use your hand or a rubber mallet to tap the lower panel's edge up, making a tight joint with the panel above it. After all of the GearWall panels are installed, screw the slotted channel track into wall studs at a height that allows long-handled tools or gear such as stepladders to hang freely. Cut the trim pieces to fit around any cutouts or openings with a utility knife.

5

6

7

8

⊳ DO IT RIGHT

Before you hang anything on the slotted panels or in the channel, confirm that there is a screw through the slotted channels at every wall stud. Follow the line of screws you installed both vertically and horizontally, and set any missing panel screws in the channel track.

⠿ DO IT FAST

Mobile GearBoxes are designed so that you can't mount their casters incorrectly; the lockable wheels are in front and the swivel wheels are in back. To further guide you, the casters align with the mounting plates on the bottom frame of the GearBoxes.

Add the Accessories

9 **BUILD THE WORKBENCH.** Follow the manufacturer's parts list and directions to assemble the 6-ft. workbench. Use the hardware provided in the package to fasten the underside of the top to the workbench frame. Once the frame is completely assembled, install casters on each leg and move the workbench into place along the wall.

10 **HANG THE GEARBOXES.** The wall-hung GearBoxes are shipped fully assembled, so all you need to do is carefully lift them into place and hook them into the slotted grooves along the panel. Adjust their locations by sliding them along the panel slots until they are positioned where you want them.

11 **PLACE THE MOBILE GEARBOXES.** Attach the casters to the mobile GearBoxes (see DO IT FAST, left) and roll them into place under the workbench flush with the wall. Lock the front casters in place to prevent them from moving.

12 **ATTACH THE ACCESSORIES.** Slide the hooks, shelf, and baskets into the panel and channel track slots. Adjust their locations for convenience, appearance, and to fit your specific tools, parts, and materials. Use the GearBoxes and accessories to store a variety of

tools and supplies (use the lockable, wall-mounted GearBoxes to keep solvents and paints out of a young child's reach), while keeping the total load within the system's 50 lbs.-per-sq.-ft. weight capacity. The configuration of the accessories can be changed over time as you acquire new tools.

9 10
11 12

Baskets, shelves, and hooks are available in kits that are less expensive in a package than as individual purchases.

The true genius of this and other modular storage solutions is the ability not only to shift the GearBoxes and accessories along the panel to suit your tools and gear, but also to add components as your needs change and your budget allows. The possible combinations are nearly endless, and the panels provide plenty of area for additional accessories and GearBoxes; there's even refrigerator-freezer units finished like the GearBox doors and drawers to help transform your garage.

Gladiator GarageWorks® offers a trio of complementary appliances, including a modular, 6-cu.-ft. refrigerator, a 21-cu.-ft. refrigerator/freezer, and a trash compactor. Make sure your garage has adequate electrical power and outlets for any appliances you add.

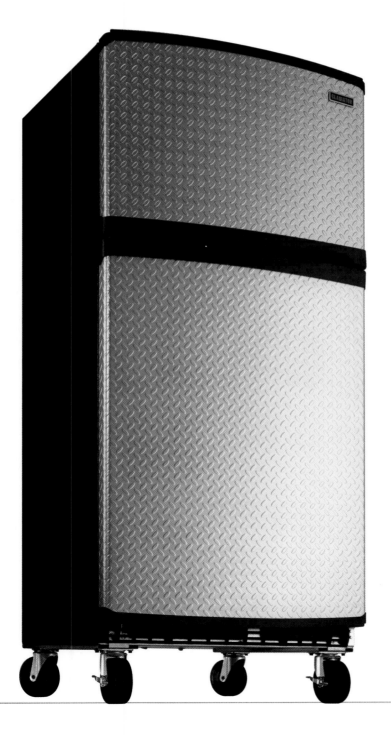

The Gladiator system includes a special hook to hang your wheelbarrow, offering an easy solution to an often awkward storage challenge. Other deep hooks support multiple long-handled tools.

Use a combination of shelves, baskets, and hangers to store yard gear, sports equipment, and seasonal items.

If your garage's space permits, extend slotted panels around its corners to another wall, and make a complete workshop for woodworking, machine, and craft projects.

The system accommodates more than just tools and yard equipment; consider attaching a vertical bike hook to the slotted panel to make efficient use of your space and keep your garage's clutter to a minimum.

Use locking Wall GearBoxes to hold garden chemicals, solvents, and other hazardous materials safely away from a child's reach.

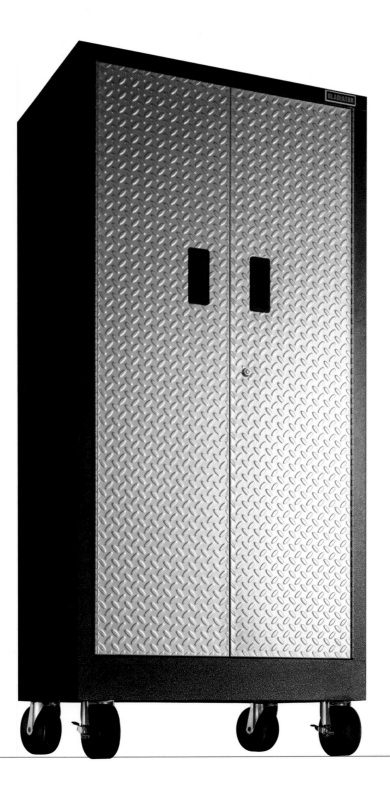

The mobile workbench is also available in an 8-ft. length, with or without casters. Its open frame construction allows cabinets and lockers to roll underneath.

The Gladiator system offers seven different GearBoxes, including a 5-ft.-tall locker (near left) and 28-in.-wide by 24-in.-deep drawer cabinet (far left)—all outfitted with lockable casters for mobility.

Overhead Organizer

Get ahead of your clutter with OVERHEAD SHELVES that take advantage of out-of-the-way space in the garage

I F YOUR GARAGE IS OVERWHELMED WITH CLUTTER, from bikes to boxes of holiday decorations, things are looking up…literally. The ceiling of your garage—including the area above your open garage doors—is the perfect spot for things you use only occasionally. In just an afternoon using a basic set of tools and prefabricated components, you can install these overhead shelves, stow away your stuff, and enjoy a garage that looks and feels more organized. Made from industrial metal and hung from the structural frame of the garage ceiling, these tough, good-looking racks can hold up to 250 lbs. of items you want to park in long-term storage.

LOCATE THE FRAMING **MOUNT THE BRACKETS** **INSTALL THE SUPPORTS** **FASTEN THE SHELVES**

▶ LINGO

Your ceiling's structural frame has many names—joist, beam, chord, and rafter—but they all mean the same thing. These generally synonymous terms identify the wooden framing members to which you'll fasten your organizer's mounting brackets and struts.

✦ DO IT NOW

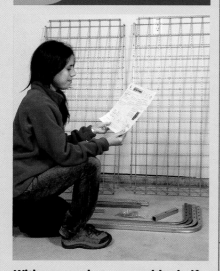

With any ready-to-assemble shelf, make sure you've got all the parts and fasteners before you start the installation. The instructions should include a complete parts list. Set aside each piece (or groups of pieces) and check their size and number against the instructions. By taking inventory, you will also get familiar with the manufacturer's lingo.

Tools & Gear

Dig through your basic tool set to find what you'll need to drill holes, assemble the organizer, and fasten it into the ceiling, including these tools:

DRILL. Use a corded or cordless drill to make pilot holes into the ceiling frame. It also will tighten the bolts and screws that hold the shelves to their supports and the brackets to the beams.

TAPE MEASURE. A retractable-steel tape measure determines the amount of clearance between the garage doors and your vehicles and measures the proper distance between the mounting brackets.

STUD FINDER. Find the location of your roofing frame's joists with this handy tool.

RUBBER MALLET. Nudge the supports into place without marring the organizer's finish.

SOCKET SET. A manual set will work fine, or get socket bits that will slip into your drill for more torque and tightening power.

STEP LADDER. Put your tools and yourself up close to the ceiling on a 6-ft. or 8-ft. stepladder.

CARPENTER'S PENCIL. Keep the tip sharp for accurate marks, especially when you locate the garage's ceiling beams.

COOL TOOL

Tape measures are all the same, right? No. It's true that they all perform the same function, but today's retractable steel tapes offer some cool features, including ergonomic molds for comfort and better grip, and they're equipped with locks that keep the extended tape in position while you mark your measurements. A tough, brightly colored housing makes the tape measure easy to find. Go for a 25-ft.-long tape to handle almost any household task or project.

What to Buy

1| READY-TO-ASSEMBLE ORGANIZERS. These self-contained, ceiling-mounted shelves come with everything you need, including support posts of different lengths that can be screwed together to accommodate different depths or telescoping supports to fit the shelves into your allowable clearances. You'll find fasteners inside the package—often even a wrench, drill bit, or a socket bit—to speed the installation. The components are all lightweight industrial metal with a bright steel or shiny white, powder-coated finish for a clean look. Assembled, the system supports up to a maximum of 250 lbs. of evenly distributed weight across standard ceiling frame designs or beam spacing.

OVERHEAD ORGANIZER DIAGRAM

Ceiling joist locations

Upper support

Joint

Shelf section

Lower support

CHECK YOUR FRAME

If your house was built before 1984, chances are good that its ceiling joists or beams are at least 2×6 lumber spaced 16 in. apart—on center—and capable of carrying quite a bit of weight; houses built after that tend to rely on 2×4 components or prefabricated, engineered trusses spaced 24 in. on center, which reduces their load-carrying ability. Check with the shelving manufacturer to make sure your garage's roof frame can handle the load, especially if you install multiple organizers or plan to store heavy items. When in doubt, restrict the load to lightweight objects, or span several joists with two 8-ft.-long, 2×4 ledger boards to spread out and share the weight across several joists.

+ WHAT CAN GO WRONG

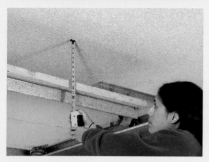

If you plan to add a shelf in the void between the top of your open overhead garage door and the ceiling, you'll need at least 19 in. of clear open space to permit usable storage without intruding on the door's operation. Also, try to avoid placing the shelves adjacent to or too close to the garage door tracks, which can limit usable storage apace.

✦ DO IT NOW

If you install your overhead shelf in a location near the garage door, test the clearance between the top of the open garage door and the ceiling before you install the shelf supports. Loosely mount a post to the first bracket you install, open the garage door, and check to make sure the door doesn't hit the post. If the clearance is okay, install the remaining mounting brackets; if not, choose another location.

Install the Shelving Unit

1 **FIND THE FRAMING.** This is easy in an open-ceiling garage. If the garage ceiling is finished with wallboard, however, use your stud finder to pinpoint the location of the ceiling's structural beams. Use a pencil to mark the outside edges of each ceiling beam every 12 in. along its length to ensure that both mounting bolts for each bracket can be fastened to the structural frame. If you have access to the attic space above the garage's ceiling, you can also climb into the space and find its beam locations.

2 **MOUNT THE BRACKETS.** With your pencil, mark the location of the overhead shelf's brackets and mounting screws, and drill pilot holes for the screws; depending on the dimensions of the shelving unit, there will be one or more mounting brackets to install on each ceiling beam. Use your socket set or a socket bit in a cordless drill to drive the screws, tightening them against the brackets.

3 **INSTALL THE SUPPORTS.** Determine the maximum length of the mounting posts to which you'll fasten the supports. If the unit uses telescoping supports, fit the pieces together, adjust their length, and insert their pins and retainer clips. For screw-together support designs, screw the supports tightly into the threaded opening in the center of each mounting bracket, then fit the shelf support  into the sleeves between two posts; if necessary, tap the sleeves with a rubber mallet. Use a tape measure to confirm that all of the supports are set at the same depth. Repeat with the second support on the other side.

4 **FASTEN THE SHELVES.** Place the shelves on top of the shelf supports, with the raised edge or lip facing down to fit snugly on the shelf supports and add structural strength. Connect the shelves to the supports using the hardware provided, following the manufacturer's directions. Load the shelves, taking care to distribute the weight of each object and the total load as evenly as possible. Check the mounting bolts at each bracket every six months and tighten them, if necessary—vibration from operating the garage door could loosen the nuts.

Some overhead racks designed for use with garage-wall panel systems are enclosed on their tops, bottoms, and sides and have an overhead door. They help keep stored goods from becoming dusty and can protect valuable items from theft.

Install two rows of overhead shelves along the perimeter sides and the end wall of your garage (left) to store heavy items that are supported by the wall's frame members rather than the ceiling joists. Compact overhead storage units (right) pull down for filling and unloading, then fold back up against the ceiling.

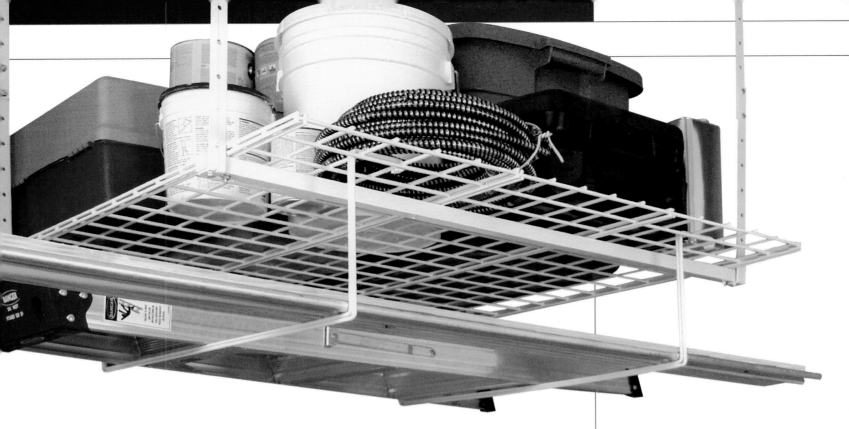

Your garage ceiling and walls can help solve your storage woes. The sky's the limit in terms of the options and accessories you can use to make your storage fit your lifestyle—and all your gear! Start by taking stock of what you have, separate it into groups by how often you need access to it—as well as by sizes and weights—and then look for storage systems and accessories that accommodate the items and your needs.

Lift bikes off the floor and out of your way—but keep them easily accessible by every member of the family. A ceiling-mounted pulley system evenly distributes the load to both wheels or the bike's frame.

If you have installed high shelves made of welded wire, use hooks to suspend items under them. It's also a great way to raise long-handled tools and sports equipment off of your garage floor.

Durable Floor Finish

Toughen up this high-traffic area with an EPOXY COATING that helps create a clean, durable & light-filled garage

NO MATTER WHAT YOU DO IN YOUR GARAGE, from car repair to carpentry, a durable, good-looking floor can help any job go a bit easier. With a few easy steps, a handful of household tools, and some rented gear, you can coat a garage floor with a good-looking epoxy finish that will stand up to just about anything you can spill on it, drive over it, or stack on top if it. Plus, the floor will be easier to keep clean, and you'll notice how the finish adds more light to your garage for greater safety and convenience.

WASH THE CONCRETE   **ETCH THE SURFACE**   **MIX THE EPOXY PAINT**   **APPLY THE FINISH**

+ SAFETY FIRST

Proper safety gear is a must for almost any project, but especially when you're dealing with chemicals and solvents. Guard against irritation with adequate eye protection, a dust mask, rubber gloves, and boots. Wear long sleeves and pants.

+ WHAT CAN GO WRONG

Standard concrete paint can be a great coating for a path, but it's no good in the garage. Simply, it tends to lift up when you roll your rig over the floor, sticking to a hot tire by reactivating the chemicals in the paint like plastic wrap clings to a hot pot. An epoxy coating, by contrast, resists lift-up.

Tools & Gear

Except for a few rented items, most of what you'll need is probably in the garage already.

OSCILLATING FAN. Even if you can facilitate cross-ventilation with doors or windows in the garage, have one of these handy to push the air around.

MASONRY TOOLS. Use a cold chisel, pointed trowel, and float to repair any cracks in the floor.

PAINT BRUSHES AND ROLLERS. Use an epoxy-rated brush and a foam or sponge-type roller to apply the paint.

FLOOR BUFFER. Rent one of these with a bristle scrubber pad to apply the muriatic acid evenly and quickly.

PRESSURE WASHER. Rent or buy this tool and attach it to a nearby garden spigot to help remove dirt, debris, or surface stains and to flush away the acid after it's applied.

CLEAN-UP ITEMS. A mist attachment for your hose, a stiff-bristled push broom, and a floor squeegee will come in handy as you prepare the surface to accept the paint.

WATERING CAN. You'll need this to safely and properly apply the muriatic acid.

GARDEN HOSE. Use with a mister nozzle to dampen the floor surface prior to painting.

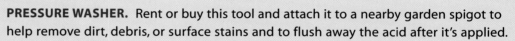

COOL TOOL

Get extra duty out of your electric drill by attaching a paint mixer bit for stirring up the two parts of your epoxy coating. Sold in various sizes to fit any handheld drill and long enough to mix a 5-gal. drum, the attachment features a design that blends the chemicals completely, helping ensure a mix that will adhere to the acid-etched surface and provide durable performance for years to come. Make sure to clean and dry the bit after use so you can use it on your next painting project.

What to Buy

1| NON-LIFTING EPOXY PAINT. A gallon of this two-part (A&B) paint with a factory-added gray or tan pigment covers about 260 sq. ft. (the size of the average two-car garage is about 575 sq. ft.). Make sure you have enough to apply two coats of relatively equal thickness. Consider adding quartz crystals after the first coat for a non-slip surface.

2| MURIATIC ACID. This industrial-strength hydrogen chloride gas, normally sold as a 30% concentrate in liquid form, will etch (or clean) the concrete surface of your garage floor in preparation for the epoxy finish. Buy only what you need (a gallon covers about 150 sq. ft.), carefully follow instructions on the container, and safely discard any leftovers, following the disposal directions on the acid container.

3| CLEANSERS. Have on hand some ammonia, either lacquer thinner or paint stripping compound, concrete spot cleaner, and tri-sodium phosphate (TSP)—along with rags and other cleaning tools—to get rid of lingering dirt, debris, paint drips, stains, and other elements that may hinder the paint from proper and lasting adhesion.

4| PATCHING CONCRETE. Use this to repair small cracks to create a smooth, level surface for the coating.

CLEAN SWEEP

Make your life a little easier by clearing your garage floor before you get started. Remove everything that isn't a permanent fixture, including refrigerator-freezers, freestanding storage cabinets, sports equipment, and tool chests. Try to have at least 6 in. of clearance below any shelving or wall-mounted storage units so you can work under them as you sweep up dirt, patch concrete, wash with muriatic acid, rinse with water, and apply paint. In addition to a shiny new floor, you may end up with less clutter!

✚ SAFETY FIRST

The chemicals you're using can be eye-watering and noxious, so make sure you provide plenty of ventilation. Open all doors and windows to catch natural cross breezes, and set up oscillating fans to move the air around and push it to the outside.

▶ DO IT RIGHT

The muriatic acid application is a two-person job: one to apply the acid, the other to follow close behind to make sure it's flushed properly before it dries. Take care to avoid splashing yourself or your helper with acid solution. Plan ahead and try a few dry runs to get a rhythm going, and work together to power wash and mop up when you're done.

▪ LINGO

To "feather" or "float" an edge on paint or patching concrete means to blend it with an existing surface where the two materials meet so that there is no raised edge between them.

Prepare the Surface

1 PUT ON THE PRESSURE. Give the garage floor a good sweeping with a stiff-bristled push broom, then power wash it to remove loose dirt, debris, and stains. With a wire brush, TSP, and water, remove stubborn stains, paint drips, and other surface blemishes. Chisel out any cracks $1/16$ in. or larger, and repair them with a patching concrete. Finish the patches by floating the patching concrete along the edges so that they're flush with the surface.

2 TEST FOR AND REMOVE SEALER. While wearing proper safety gear, dilute 1 part of muriatic acid with 1 part of water in a plastic cup according to the manufacturer's directions, and pour the solution over a small area of the floor. If it does not bubble on contact, your floor is sealed and needs to be sanded before you etch the floor to allow proper epoxy adhesion. Flush the acid before it dries, usually within 10 minutes.

3 ETCH THE SURFACE. Remove or protect any non-plastic surfaces from the acid, and put on your protective gear, making sure none of the skin on your arms or legs is exposed. In a watering can, add equal parts acid and water—adding the acid to the water so as not to splatter acid and damage the watering can. Apply the solution to an 8-ft.-square area and use the buffer to spread it

evenly, working in two passes at right angles to each other. Treat the next 8-ft. section while your helper rinses off the acid layer before it dries.

4 CLEAN UP FOR THE COATING. Use a stiff broom to apply ammonia to clean the entire area and neutralize any remaining acid, then rinse the surface with your pressure washer. Rinse the surface again if you see a dusty residue after the concrete dries. Use a squeegee to push any standing water or puddles out of the garage and onto the driveway.

1

2

3

4

✓ UPGRADE

You can create a non-slip surface by adding a traction agent you mix into the epoxy itself. Another option is a layer of quartz-based crystals or granules over the first coat of paint before it cures. Wear spiked or cleated shoes when spreading the crystals (follow the manufacturer's directions). The finish coat covers the quartz and leaves a textured surface with good traction, though it also will be a bit harder to sweep.

✛ WHAT CAN GO WRONG

If you allow the first coat of epoxy to completely cure—typically longer than 48 hours—you'll need a floor sander to abrade the surface so it will accept the finish coat and still adhere properly between the two layers.

▸ LINGO

"Crosshatching" is an application technique. Within a selected area, spread the coating left to right, then front to back (or perpendicular) before moving on to the next section.

Mix & Apply the Epoxy

5 **MIX IT UP.** For best result, plan your project when the concrete floor surface temperature is at least 50°F, and keep the surface damp with a moist rag as you apply the paint. Before you blend the two parts (clearly marked A & B), use your drill and mixer bit to thoroughly stir Part A. Then pour Part B into Part A's container and mix the two compounds to make paint of a honey-like consistency. Don't mix more epoxy than you can use in a 2-hour period, and clean your mixer attachment immediately.

6 **SPREAD IT OUT.** Use a brush to apply the first (or primer) coat of epoxy around the perimeter of the garage and feather it out 6 in. to 8 in. from the edges. Pour a quarter of the epoxy into a standard paint tray or in a line across the floor and use your roller to apply the epoxy in a crosshatch pattern over the main area. Once the  entire floor is covered, allow it to dry (or cure) overnight. Press your gloved palm into the surface; if your handprint remains, wait a few more hours—but no longer than 48 hours since applying the primer coat—to apply the finish coat.

7 **PREP FOR THE FINISH.** Once the first coat of epoxy is dry, sweep it off with a stiff bristle broom or use a paint scraper to remove any dust, dirt, or other debris before applying the finish coat. As with the first coat, mix enough epoxy as you can use in two hours or less (see Step 5, above). Dampen the surface of the concrete with a hose and a mister before you apply the paint.

8 **LET IT CURE.** Apply the finish coat using the same approach as you used for Step 6. Allow the surface to dry (or cure) for 48 hours before walking on it, and at least four days before putting your vehicles and gear back into the garage. During that time, thoroughly clean your tools. Dispose of any leftover epoxy compound or empty paint containers at your nearest hazardous materials collection center.

5

6

7

8

Do-it-yourselfers can find epoxy garage floor finishing systems as individual items or as a complete kit. The kit contains a heavy-duty cleaner, the two-part epoxy paint, quartz crystals for adding texture to the floor, plus directions.

Tough, flexible, and non-porous PVC quickly covers a garage floor. Simply piece interlocking tiles together (above) or roll a mat over the existing surface and cut it to fit with scissors (right), and you're ready to drive into the garage.

There's more than one way to create a bright, clean, and safe floor surface for your garage. Some materials and methods are even easier—though less durable—than applying a two-coat epoxy paint; it all depends on your budget, the look you want, how you use your garage, and how permanent the solution needs to be. A modular, roll-out plastic surface, for instance, might be perfect for a small area of the garage, while rubber tiles enable you to get creative with colors and patterns. Some surfaces allow you to create lines or boundaries for indoor sports or other activities when the vehicles are in the driveway, while paint coatings are available in a variety of surface treatments for a unique look.

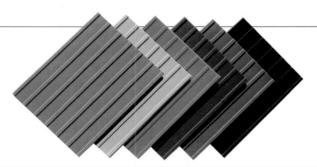

Rubber mats serve small and specific areas of the garage. Their rubber backing sticks to the concrete, while their surface can range from hard plastic to the feel of carpet or fabric.

Accessorize your new floor with parking stops and garage door thresholds to achieve the look you like and the ultimate in convenience and climate protection.

An interlocking grid system of 2-ft.-square polypropylene tiles allows creative surface patterns and color combinations.

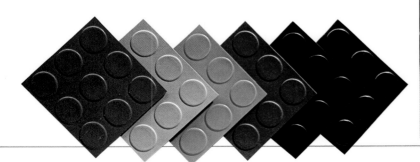

Lighting Upgrade

Add efficient, high-output LIGHT FIXTURES inside and outside your garage to boost visibility, safety & security

I F YOU'RE TIRED OF RELYING ON A SINGLE, 60-WATT BULB to find your way around the garage, help is only a project away. Replacing incandescent bulbs with fluorescent light fixtures will provide about six times the amount of light—and more safely and with far less energy. You'll notice an immediate improvement in your ability to work and find things in the garage. But why stop there? Just outside every entrance to your house, including the side door to the garage, is an incandescent light in need of an upgrade to a halogen floodlight controlled by a motion sensor. This device not only delivers more light, but also adds a security barrier and boosts the energy efficiency and life of the bulb.

REMOVE THE OLD FIXTURE	HANG THE NEW FIXTURE	INSTALL A FIXTURE BRACKET	ADJUST THE OUTPUT

⫶▶ LINGO

The UL label on fixtures, bulbs, and other electrical components denotes that they have been tested and approved for performance at their intended use by Underwriter's Laboratories, an independent, non-profit agency.

⊛ WHAT'S DIFFERENT?

Fluorescent fixtures are sold as RS (rapid-start), IS (instant-start), or S (Starter) types. The difference is the location of the starter that delivers an electrical charge to the tubes. RS fixtures have their starters in their ballasts; their lamps come on as you flip the switch. On IS and S fixtures, the starter and ballast are separate.

✦ DO IT NOW

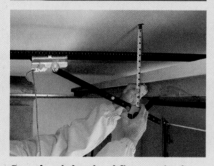

Buy the right-sized fixtures by first measuring the clearances from other protruding elements on the ceiling of the garage, such as tracks, drives, and motors of automatic garage door openers; heating ducts; and lights. You'll avoid getting a fixture that's too big for the space.

Tools & Gear

Rely on hand tools for this job, as they are easier to manage in tall, tight spaces.

STUD FINDER. A battery-powered stud finder offers an easy and reliable way to locate ceiling joists for hanging fluorescent fixtures and wall frames for wall fixtures.

SCREWDRIVERS. Keep both a Phillips and a flat-head screwdriver handy.

PLIERS. A pair of needlenose and lineman's pliers are essential for pulling and twisting wires.

TAPE MEASURE AND PENCIL. You'll need both to check clearances and distances; always keep the pencil's tip sharp.

VOLTAGE TESTER. Use this tool to make sure power is off before you work and flowing to the fixture before you finish the job.

WIRE STRIPPER. Find a tool you can use on wires of various-sizes (see COOL TOOL, below).

STEPLADDER. A stable platform and integral shelf is essential to working safely.

CORDLESS DRILL. This will make short work of drilling pilot holes and mounting screws.

GLOVES. Thin cloth or latex gloves should be worn when installing halogen bulbs.

COOL TOOL

The latest generation of wire strippers make it easy to cut and cleanly strip (or remove) a wire's insulated vinyl coating, revealing the bare wire. Without adjustment, these tools clamp their metal jaws around a 2-in. or smaller section of wire; a gentle tug and the bare wire is cleanly revealed. The trigger action also controls a wire cutter located under the jaws that snips cables to the size you need.

What to Buy

1| RAPID-START FLUORESCENT FIXTURE. Depending on what size fixture your ceiling can accommodate (see WHAT CAN GO WRONG, p. 114), get one with a single or dual bulb capacity that either hangs from chains or attaches directly to the ceiling joists (or indirectly to them after passing through the wallboard). Rapid-start units illuminate when you flip the switch. Make sure you purchase rapid-start bulbs—or lamps and tubes—too.

2| HALOGEN FLOODLIGHT FIXTURE. This is a self-contained fixture that features either a one- or two-lamp design depending on how much area you want to cover with illumination and all the mounting hardware you'll need; get one with an integral daylight sensor that turns the motion sensor on at dusk and off at dawn.

3| ELECTRICAL TAPE. A roll of this is always handy for wire repairs, splices, connections, and waterproofing.

4| MOUNTING STRAP AND NIPPLE/STUD. Have these on hand for one or both fixtures to retrofit the junction box if necessary (see the illustration below).

5| WIRE NUTS. These connectors are used to join two wire ends and protect the splice.

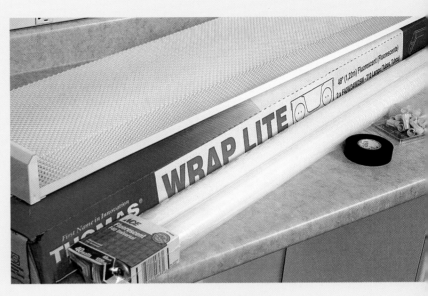

ANATOMY OF A FIXTURE

Generally, all light fixtures feature the same basic components, including: the junction box or receptacle (A), stud, mounting plate, or mounting strap (B), locknut (C), the housing or mount of the fixture (D), a white neutral wire (E) that carriers power back to the service panel, a black live or hot wire (F) that brings power from the service panel, and a green or bare ground wire (G) that you attach to a screw inside the housing. Always connect the wires white to white, black to black, and green to metal housing or box.

✛ WHAT CAN GO WRONG

If your lamps flicker or don't turn on properly, check to make sure they are properly seated in their holders by carefully rotating them. Also check for damaged pins at the ends of the lamp tubes, as well as discolored lamps, both of which may indicate conditions that hinder their ability to light properly.

▸ LINGO

The ballast is the heart of every fluorescent light fixture. It is an electrical transformer that steps up the voltage from the main line and sends that high-voltage current to the lamp holders to activate the tubes.

A New Fluorescent Fixture

1 **OUT WITH THE OLD.** Find the breaker or fuse at the service panel for the circuit that provides power to the incandescent bulb fixture you are replacing, and turn off the breaker or remove the fuse. Remove the fixture's bulb and use the voltage tester to confirm the power is off. Expose the wires between the fixture and the junction box, and unscrew or detach the fixture. Separate the wires, reactivate the circuit, and test the wires with a voltage tester to confirm full current, then cut the power again. Wrap bare—or exposed—wires with electrical tape, leaving the last 1½ in. of each wire bare.

2 **MOUNT THE FIXTURE.** Locate the two nearest wooden ceiling joists with your stud finder. If the junction box has no fixture-mounting strap, screw a round mounting plate to it and thread the wires through the hole. Holding the fixture in place, thread the wires through the mounting hole in the new fixture and loosely secure it in place with the provided locknut. Adjust the fixture so that each mounting hole aligns  under a joist. Mark the hole's location with a pencil, drill pilot holes into the joist, mount the fixture with its provided screws, and tighten the locknut.

3 **CONNECT THE WIRES.** Other wires may be present, but look for a bundled cable of white, black, and bare or green grounding wires. Strip 1½ in. of insulation from the ends of each wire. Connect the wires—black to black, white to white, and green to the junction box grounding screw, twisting each wire pair inside a wire nut. Restore power, and test that power is flowing through the fixture with a voltage tester.

4 **INSTALL THE LAMPS.** Line up the pins of the bulb(s) with their holders, press them into place, and rotate them until they lock. Test the light fixture to make sure it's operating properly.

▶ DO IT RIGHT

Wait until dark to set and test the angle and span of the motion sensor. You'll want the angle to be set slightly smaller than its maximum to prevent activation when pets pass by, but not so far as to miss a human's presence. Adjust the span to capture people when they're at least 15 ft. from the area protected by the security light.

+ WHAT CAN GO WRONG

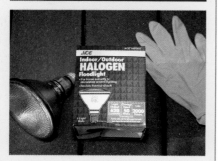

Halogen lamps cost more than incandescent bulbs, but they last longer. Avoid touching an exposed halogen lamp; the oils from your skin can cause the lamp to prematurely deteriorate, lessen its usable life, and lead to premature failure.

A New Motion-Sensor Light

1 **REMOVE THE EXISTING FIXTURE.** Find the circuit on the service panel that provides power to the fixture to be replaced, and turn off the breaker or remove the fuse. While on your stepladder, carefully remove the bulb and fixture to expose the wires and junction box, use the voltage tester to confirm that the power is off, and remove the old fixture. Separate the bare wires, reactivate the circuit, and test them with your voltage tester to confirm full current, then turn the power back off. Wrap exposed wires with electrical tape, leaving the last 1½ in. of each wire bare.

2 **CONNECT THE FIXTURE.** Separate the white, black, and bare or green grounding wires. Strip 1½ in. of insulation from the ends of each wire. Connect the wires—black to black, white to white, and ground to the junction box grounding screw. Twist the two ends of each wire pair together with a wire nut, reactivate the circuit, and use the voltage tester to confirm that power is flowing to and from the fixture. Turn off the power, then connect each wire pair with a wire nut and cover them with electrical tape to waterproof the splice.

3 **MOUNT THE FIXTURE.** Fold the connected wires into the junction box and place the fixture housing over it to align with the mounting holes of the junction box. Mount the fixture directly to the box with the screws provided (if the fixture's holes do not match up, first screw a mounting strap for the fixture onto the junction box, then attach the fixture to the mounting strap). All of the wires should be completely contained and protected by the fixture housing.

4 **INSTALL THE BULB.** Wearing lightweight gloves, install the fixture's halogen bulb(s), seal the housing, reactivate the circuit, and test the light at night using the switch. Leave the switch in the "on" position and remain motionless; the light will turn off in a few minutes, then reactivate when you move. Adjust the motion sensor, as necessary, following the manufacturer's instructions (see DO IT RIGHT, left).

1

2

3

4

If you already have a porch light outside a side or other door to the house or garage, consider retrofitting it with a motion sensor that simply mounts to the wall and connects between the bulb and the lamp housing.

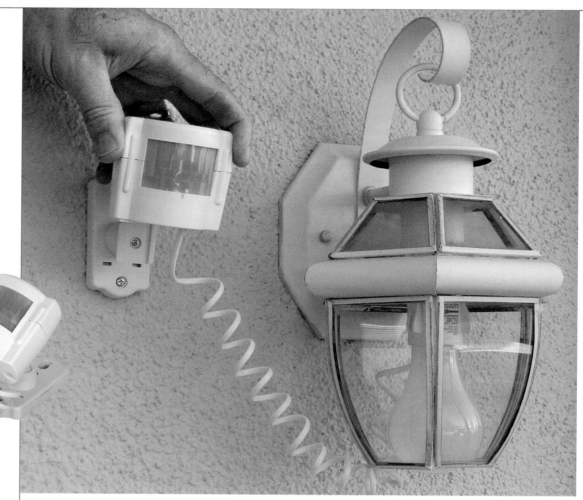

You'll be amazed at how much better

your garage looks and feels with more light, such as overhead fluorescent fixtures and bench-mounted or counter-height task lighting. You can even use spotlight fixtures to showcase a classic car, a tool rack, or a storage area. In addition, properly designed lighting makes for a safer and more comfortable work area. You'll save energy and extend lamp life by adding motion sensors that activate your lights when you walk into the garage and then turn off automatically.

For extra bright illumination and cost savings, use a metal-halide fixture as your general light source. It delivers a brighter, more natural color than fluorescent lamps. Halide lamps take a few minutes to warm up to full intensity.

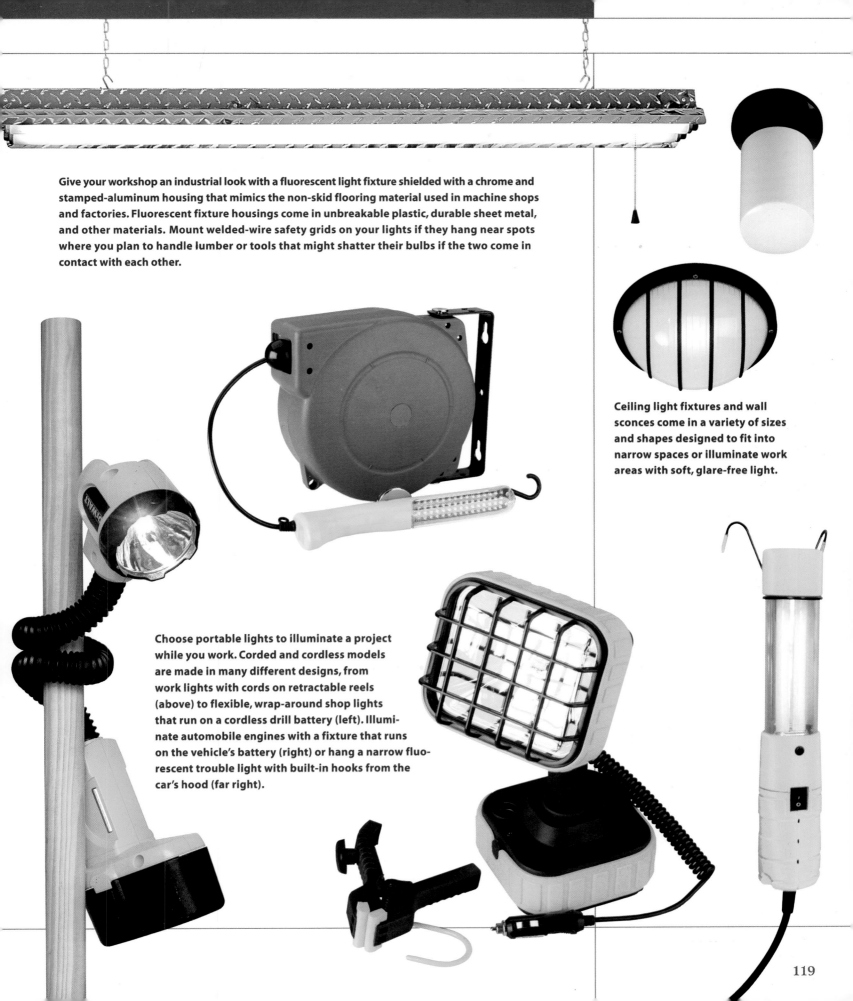

Give your workshop an industrial look with a fluorescent light fixture shielded with a chrome and stamped-aluminum housing that mimics the non-skid flooring material used in machine shops and factories. Fluorescent fixture housings come in unbreakable plastic, durable sheet metal, and other materials. Mount welded-wire safety grids on your lights if they hang near spots where you plan to handle lumber or tools that might shatter their bulbs if the two come in contact with each other.

Ceiling light fixtures and wall sconces come in a variety of sizes and shapes designed to fit into narrow spaces or illuminate work areas with soft, glare-free light.

Choose portable lights to illuminate a project while you work. Corded and cordless models are made in many different designs, from work lights with cords on retractable reels (above) to flexible, wrap-around shop lights that run on a cordless drill battery (left). Illuminate automobile engines with a fixture that runs on the vehicle's battery (right) or hang a narrow fluorescent trouble light with built-in hooks from the car's hood (far right).

Photo Credits

All photographs by John Rickard, except:

Jerry Bates: p. 9: (top left), p. 26: (both), p. 27: (top), p. 52: (both), p. 53: (top, bottom right), p. 76: (top left, top right), p. 77: (top right, bottom right), p. 109: (top left, bottom left), p. 112: (bottom left), p. 118: (top, inset), p. 119: (top left, bottom left)

Robert J. Dolezal: p. 106: (top left), p. 108: (top left)

Other photographs courtesy of:

p. i: Schulte Corporation
p. iii: Gladiator GarageWorks
p. v: Griot's Garage (top left); Schulte Corporation (top right)
p. 2: Garage Tek (top left)
p. 27: Improvements (bottom left); Home Focus (bottom right)
p. 28: All Bright Ideas (bottom); Garage Tek (top)
p. 29: All Bright Ideas (bottom right); Schulte Corporation (top, bottom left)
p. 38: Gladiator GarageWorks (bottom left)
p. 40: Garage Tek (middle left); Improvements (top right); Home Focus (bottom right)
p. 41: Garage Tek (top left, top right); Schulte Corporation (bottom left, bottom right)

p. 64: Garage Tek (bottom right); Schulte Corporation (top left); Sporty's Tool Shop (bottom left)
p. 65: Griot's Garage (all)
p. 76: Improvements (bottom)
p. 77: Plow & Hearth (left)
pp. 80–91: Gladiator GarageWorks (all)
p. 98: Better Life Technologies (bottom right); Garage Tek (top); Hyloft (bottom left)
p. 99: Improvements (middle); Hyloft (top, bottom)
p. 102: Racedeck (bottom left)
p. 108: Gladiator GarageWorks (bottom left, bottom right)
p. 109: Improvements (top right, right inset, bottom right); Racedeck (middle left)
p. 119: Lighting Universe (top, middle right); Northern Tool & Equipment (center, bottom middle, bottom right)